lulu on the bridge

lulu
on the
bridge

A FILM BY

Paul Auster

An Owl Book

Henry Holt and Company • New York

Henry Holt and Company, Inc.
Publishers since 1866
115 West 18th Street
New York, New York 10011

Henry Holt ® is a registered trademark of
Henry Holt and Company, Inc.

Published in Canada by Fitzhenry & Whiteside Ltd.
195 Allstate Parkway, Markham, Ontario L3R 4T8

Library of Congress Cataloging-in-Publication Data
Auster, Paul, 1947–
Lulu on the bridge: a film by Paul Auster.
p.   cm.
"An Owl Book."
ISBN 0-8050-5978-4 (pbk.: alk. paper)
1. Lulu on the bridge (Motion picture) I. Title.
PN1997.L85A98 1998   98-17750
791.43'72—dc21   CIP

Henry Holt books are available for special promotions and
premiums. For details contact: Director, Special Markets.

First Edition 1998

Designed by Kelly Soong

Printed in the United States of America
All first editions are printed on acid-free paper.

1   3   5   7   9   10   8   6   4   2

contents

lulu on the bridge

Written and Directed by
Paul Auster

Producers
Peter Newman, Greg Johnson, Amy Kaufman

Director of Photography
Alik Sakharov

Editor
Tim Squyres

Production Designer
Kalina Ivanov

Costume Designer
Adelle Lutz

Music
Graeme Revell

Executive Producers
Sharon Harel, Jane Barclay, Ira Deutchman

Still Photographer
Abbot Genser

CAST

(In order of appearance)

Izzy Maurer	**Harvey Keitel**
Dave Reilly	**Richard Edson**
Young Man	**Nick Sandow**
Young Woman	**Mel Gorham**
Tyrone Lord	**Don Byron**
Man with Gun	**Kevin Corrigan**
Celia Burns	**Mira Sorvino**
Pierre	**Victor Argo**
Dr. Fischer	**Peggy Gormley**
Bobby Perez	**Harold Perrineau**
Hannah	**Gina Gershon**
Sonia Kleinman	**Sophie Auster**
Catherine Moore	**Vanessa Redgrave**
Philip Kleinman	**Mandy Patinkin**
Stanley Mar	**Greg Johnson**
Laughing Man Escort	**David Byrne**
Dying Girl	**Holly Buczek**
Not Lou Reed	**Lou Reed**
Restaurant Man #1	**Tom Gilroy**
Restaurant Man #2	**Paul Lazar**
Restaurant Man #3	**Michael Ceveris**
Russian Thug	**Slava Schoot**
Chinese Thug	**Henry Yuk**
German Thug	**Fred Norris**
Black	**Giancarlo Esposito**
Dr. Van Horn	**Willem Dafoe**
Alvin Shine	**Jared Harris**
Peter Shine	**Josef Sommer**
Molly	**Cara Buono**
Candy	**Karen Sillas**
Jack	**David Thornton**
First Pursuer	**Brian McGuiness**
Second Pursuer	**Neil Donovan**
Paramedic #1	**Socorro Santiago**
Paramedic #2	**O. L. Duke**

What follows is the entire shooting script of *Lulu on the Bridge*. In the final version of the film, a number of scenes were either shortened or eliminated. The complete cast is listed in the credits.

lulu on the bridge

1. INT: NIGHT. NEW YORK JAZZ CLUB. THE MEN'S ROOM.

Crowd noise outside. Two hundred people clapping rhythmically, urging the featured group to come out on stage. Chanting: Kat-man-du. Kat-man-du.

IZZY MAURER, a jazz veteran in his late forties or early fifties, is peeing into one of the urinals. We see him from behind. It is an old place, with crumbling plaster and paint peeling from the walls. On the wall directly in front of him, Scotch-taped above the urinals in haphazard fashion, are photographs of various movie actresses cut out from newspapers and magazines: Louise Brooks, Ingrid Bergman, Jean Harlow, Ava Gardner, Grace Kelly, Vanessa Redgrave, Isabella Rossellini, Mira Sorvino, and others. The camera scans the faces of the movie stars. Reverse angle: close-up of IZZY's face studying the photos as he pees.

DAVE REILLY, a member of the band, opens the door and pokes his head into the men's room. A bit frantic.

DAVE

There you are. Come on, Izzy, let's go. They're waiting for us.

IZZY

(*Still peeing*) Just a second. I can't go on with my dick hanging out, can I? (*Finishes. Zips up his pants*)

Cut to:

2. INT: NIGHT. NEW YORK JAZZ CLUB. HALLWAY.

IZZY steps out of the men's room into the corridor. The crowd noise increases. Two patrons of the club—a YOUNG MAN and YOUNG WOMAN—happen to be walking by. The space is so narrow that IZZY can't get past them. An awkward, indecisive moment: the man accidentally bumps into IZZY.

IZZY

(*Irritated*) Watch it.

YOUNG MAN

Sorry. (*Realizing who it is*) Jesus, you're Izzy Maurer, aren't you?

IZZY

Out of my way, kid. I've got to go on. (*The noise of the crowd swells*) Are you deaf?

YOUNG MAN

I just want you to know that I'm a big fan. I've been following your stuff for years.

YOUNG WOMAN

(*Equally impressed*) It's true. This is like, a big moment for him, you know?

IZZY

Well, it's not a big moment for me.

Both the YOUNG MAN and YOUNG WOMAN react to IZZY's cruelty with hurt, bewildered looks. IZZY begins pushing his way around them.

Noticing that the YOUNG WOMAN is attractive, he pauses for a moment to look her up and down as he slides past.

DAVE

(*From the other end of the corridor*) Izzy! Come on!

Shot of IZZY from behind, walking quickly down the tunnel-like corridor toward DAVE, who is standing at the end, bathed in light. Cut to:

3. INT: NIGHT. JAZZ CLUB. THE STAGE.

Katmandu performs. There are six musicians in the group. IZZY plays the saxophone. He is the lead performer.

It is a large place: high ceiling, murky light, customers sitting at tables with drinks in front of them. Then, just as the tempo quickens, a disturbance is heard in the far corner of the room (off camera). A man is shouting. People are starting to scream.

IZZY, oblivious to the commotion, goes on playing with his eyes closed—lost in the music. The MAN comes into view—lurching, possessed, a gun in his right hand.

MAN

Nancy! Nancy! God wants it this way, Nancy! We're going to burn in hell, Nancy! You and me and God—all of us together!

He fires off a wild shot. The bullet goes into the ceiling. Chunks of plaster rain down. The MAN *runs past the stage, looking for* NANCY. *The drummer and the pianist stop playing.* IZZY *continues, eyes still closed. Confusion, alarm, people getting up and running headlong for the exits. Chairs are overturned, bodies collide. Fast cuts. Zoom: the* MAN *spots* NANCY, *terrified, getting up from her seat.* ANOTHER MAN *is with her, his arm around her shoulder.*

MAN *(cont'd)*

(*Taking aim*) God wants it this way, Nancy! You belong to me—not to him—not to anyone but me!

IZZY's *eyes finally open. An instant later, the gun goes off.* IZZY *is hit. The bullet goes through his left hand and then into his chest. Blood begins to spread across his shirt. We see the* MAN *rush toward* NANCY *in the upper left-hand corner of the screen. He shoots her, shoots the man she is with, and then, howling, turns the gun on himself and puts a bullet through his own head.*

Meanwhile . . . IZZY, *gravely wounded, staggers for a moment and then topples off the stage to the floor.* TYRONE LORD, *the black drummer,*

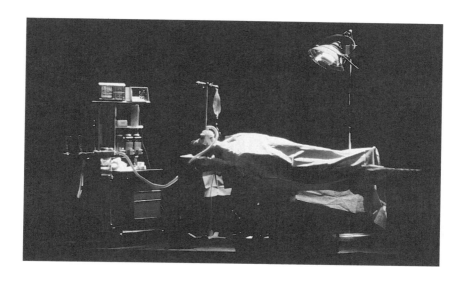

leaps off the stage. He crouches beside IZZY *and clamps his hands over the wound.*

IZZY *is lying on his back.* IZZY'S POV: *we see a small chunk of plaster come loose from the ceiling and fall through the air. Close-up of* IZZY'S *face: his eyes close. Cut to:*

4. INT: NIGHT. HOSPITAL OPERATING ROOM.

IZZY, *breathing through tubes, is lying on a hospital bed, surrounded by black limbo. Sounds of the respirator.*

5. EXT: DAY. NEW YORK STREET.

Late afternoon, autumn. An attractive young woman, CELIA BURNS, *is walking down the street. She enters a French restaurant: Chez Pierre.*

6. INT: DAY. CHEZ PIERRE.

It is an hour or so before dinnertime. Busboys are setting up the tables. PIERRE, *the owner, a man in his fifties, is sitting at one of the tables, drinking an espresso and smoking a cigarette. He is reading the* New York Post. *We see the front-page headline: "IZZY LIVES! Jazzman survives 7-hour oper-ation. Left Lung Removed."*

He glimpses CELIA *over the top of his paper. Casually, but with affection. He clearly has something of a crush on her.*

PIERRE

Hi there, pretty one.

CELIA

(*Stops*) Hi, Pierre. (*Beat*) I was wondering . . . (*Is about to say something, but is distracted by the newspaper headline*) He made it. I'm glad.

PIERRE

(*Momentarily confused, then catches on. Turns the paper around*) Yeah, he made it. But the article says he'll probably never play again. A one-lunged saxophonist with a broken hand. Doesn't sound too hopeful, does it?

CELIA

Did you ever hear him play?

PIERRE

Nah. I'm not too big on jazz. Give me Chuck Berry any day.

CELIA

I hear it's good.

PIERRE

They say there's been a big run on Katmandu's last CD.

CELIA

That's good.

PIERRE

Good? I'd call it pretty ironic. The guy plays for years, and nobody's ever heard of him. Then he gets shot, his career is destroyed, and sud-denly he's a success.

At least he's alive. You can't do anything unless you're alive. (*Starts walking toward the back of the restaurant*)

PIERRE

Celia.

CELIA

(*Stops*) Yes?

PIERRE

Weren't you going to say something?

CELIA

(*Laughs*) I completely forgot. (*Taps her head*) I have an audition next Tuesday. I wondered if I could work dinner instead of lunch.

PIERRE

Arrange it with Bob or Helen. If they're not willing to switch, the answer's no. If they are, then no problem.

CELIA

Okay. Fair enough. (*Starts walking away again*)

PIERRE

(*Turns back to the newspaper. Then, over his shoulder*) What's the part?

CELIA

A shampoo commercial.

PIERRE

Are you the before or the after?

CELIA

Probably neither. I don't think I'll get it.

PIERRE

Of course you will. It's in the bag.

CELIA

(*Smiles, touches her head*) Not enough hair.

True enough, her hair is rather short.

7. INT: DAY. THE HOSPITAL. A DOUBLE ROOM.

Some days later. IZZY *is in bed, heavily bandaged around the chest. His left arm is in a sling; there is a cast on his left hand.* DR. FISCHER, *a psychotherapist in her forties, is sitting in a chair beside the bed. A pen in her right hand, a yellow legal pad on her lap. The curtain around* IZZY's *bed has been closed, giving the scene a tight, claustrophobic feel.*

DR. FISCHER

So there's no point in discussing it. Is that what you think?

IZZY

How can I discuss something I can't even remember?

DR. FISCHER

That's normal. Memory loss is perfectly normal in cases like these.

IZZY

Fuck normal. Is that the only word you people know around here? I don't give a shit about normal.

DR. FISCHER

You're angry. And why shouldn't you be? A total stranger almost killed you—for no reason at all. If I were in your shoes, I'd be angry, too.

IZZY

You still don't get it. I'm not angry because I was shot. That's the one part of the business I'm willing to accept.

DR. FISCHER

I see. So getting shot was "just one of those things." Is that what you're telling me?

IZZY

Look, it's a crazy world out there, lady. Lunatics on the prowl, a gun in every pocket, and who am I to think that one of them couldn't be turned against my poor carcass? Just read the papers. The American sky is dark with ammo, and every seventeen minutes, another person gets hit.

DR. FISCHER

What are you trying to say?

IZZY

That those are the breaks. If I could go back to my old life, I wouldn't feel so bad. I'd shrug it off, get on with playing my sax, and that would be that. As it is, the moment I leave this hospital, I'm nowhere.

DR. FISCHER

You're alive. Don't ever forget that. You're alive, and by the time you get out of here, you'll be in reasonably good physical shape. Everything else is secondary. It might take a while for you to figure

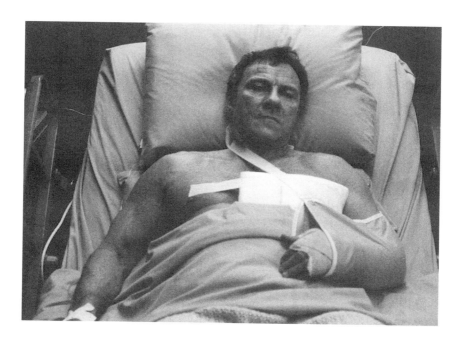

out your next move, but you start with life. And life is a beautiful thing, Mr. Maurer.

IZZY

No it's not. Life is life, and it's only beautiful if you make it beautiful. I wish I could say I've done that, but I can't. The only beautiful thing I've ever done is play music. If I can't have that, I might as well be dead. Am I making myself clear? I'd rather have lost both my legs or both my eyes than my left lung. A lung equals breath. Breath equals music. Music equals life. Without music, I have no life.

DR. FISCHER

You talk like someone who feels he's been punished.

IZZY

Well, maybe I have. A madman fires a bullet into my body, and justice is finally done.

DR. FISCHER

Then what about all that crazy world stuff? If you accept what happened as a random, arbitrary event, then you can't turn around and tell me it was done on purpose. It's got to be one or the other. You can't have it both ways.

IZZY

I can't, huh? And what if I feel like contradicting myself? Who's going to stop me?

DR. FISCHER

All right, contradict yourself. Let's say you were punished. In fact, let's go one step further and say that you deserved to be punished. If that's the case, then my question to you would be: who did the punishing?

IZZY

(Shrugs. Defensive) How should I know?

12

DR. FISCHER

Come, come, Mr. Maurer, you can do better than that. Who did the punishing?

IZZY

God. It has to be God, doesn't it? I mean, who else can punish a person like that?

DR. FISCHER

Are you telling me you believe in God?

IZZY

No, Frau Doktor, that's not what I'm telling you. I don't believe in anything.

8. INT: DAY. CELIA'S APARTMENT. WEST TWENTY-FIFTH STREET.

CELIA lives in a simple one-bedroom apartment in Chelsea. She enters with a purse slung over her shoulder and a yellow plastic bag from Tower Records in

one hand. She flings her purse onto the sofa and walks over to a small table on which there is an inexpensive portable CD/tape player. She slides her hand into the bag and pulls out the Katmandu CD. She begins trying to remove the clear plastic wrapper and finds it exceedingly difficult. Her fingernails can't get a purchase on it. She mutters under her breath, exasperated. Finally, unable to get the wrapper off with her hands, she puts the CD in her mouth and begins using her teeth.

After much effort, a slit is opened, and she finishes the job with her fingers, carefully peeling the silver seal from the edge of the jewel box. Once this long comedy of frustration is over, she takes out the CD and inserts it in the machine. She pushes a button and the music begins. The camera moves up to her face. We see her listening. Thoughtful.

9. INT: DAY. IZZY'S APARTMENT. PERRY STREET.

The music continues to play. . . .

We see IZZY *sitting in an armchair in the living room of his small, cramped apartment on Perry Street. His saxophone case lies on the floor, unopened. He stares at it as if it were a dead animal. Under the music, we hear the telephone ring.* IZZY *makes no move to answer it. After a moment, we hear* IZZY's *voice saying:*

IZZY'S VOICE

Leave a message, and I'll get back to you.

Then, after the beep:

MALE VOICE

Izzy, it's Dave again. Come on, man, don't do this to me. We gotta talk. You hear me? Don't be a schmuck, Izzy. (*Beat*) Just remember who your friends are, okay?

The receiver clicks. A moment later, the phone rings again. We hear IZZY's *voice ("leave a message, and I'll get back to you"), a beep, and then another message. As it plays, IZZY sighs, gets up from his chair, and leaves the apartment. He moves with great difficulty. He is weak, disoriented, barely able to put one foot in front of the other without losing his balance.*

FEMALE VOICE

Izzy, pick up the damn phone. It's Hannah, for Chrissakes. Remember me? We used to be married. Back in the old days. When knights were brave and chicks were bold . . . and bullets weren't invented. (*Beat*) Give me a call, Maurer, I want to know how you're doing.

By the time the message is over, IZZY has already left the apartment. The empty room and the voice.

Then, after the click, cut to:

10. EXT: DAY. STREET MONTAGE.

The music continues to play . . .

We see IZZY stumbling around the streets of the West Village. Handheld camera. Perceptual wobbles. Tops of buildings, sky, clouds, shuffling feet. Colors fade

in and out. Overexposures, underexposures, glinting light. A sense of mixed-up signals and crossed mental wires. IZZY's attention is momentarily caught by isolated objects and colors: a green scarf wrapped around a woman's neck, for example, or the red taillight of a passing taxi. The world in fragments. He gets tangled up in a dog leash, bumps into a trash can. And yet, through it all, a sense of earnest struggle, no self-pity.

He moves with the determination and courage of a small child learning how to walk—or an old man refusing to give up.

A number of passersby seem to recognize IZZY. By now, after all, he has become a famous New York figure. We see one shaking his hand and patting him on the shoulder, as if wishing him luck. IZZY looks down, nodding vaguely, unable to engage himself in the conversation.

Finally, he enters the White Horse Tavern. The moment he opens the door, the music stops. Crowd noises from within.

11. INT: DAY. THE WHITE HORSE TAVERN.

An hour or two later. IZZY is seated at a corner table with a stack of newspapers piled high in front of him: the New York dailies, the Village Voice, *the* Observer, *the* Amsterdam News. *He is sipping a cold drink and reading a copy of* Newsday. *Utterly absorbed.*

BOBBY PEREZ, a casually dressed man in his mid-thirties, approaches the table.

BOBBY

Hi, Izzy.

IZZY doesn't look up; goes on reading his paper.

BOBBY (cont'd)

Hi, Izzy. How're you doing?

IZZY looks up. From his expression, it is clear that he doesn't recognize the man.

BOBBY (*cont'd*)

Bobby Perez. I did the sound at your Summer Stage gig last year. (*Still not much of a response. Beat*) We were all rooting for you, Iz. I'm really glad you pulled through.

IZZY

Thanks, Billy. I'm doing much better now. I think I'm a lot younger than I was the last time you saw me.

BOBBY

(*A little confused*) Wow. Yeah, probably. I see what you mean.

IZZY

And I forgot to put on my watch this morning. (*Holds up his left wrist to demonstrate*) See? No watch. I consider that progress, real progress.

12. INT: DAY. IZZY'S APARTMENT. THE BEDROOM.

Seven-thirty in the morning. IZZY *is sleeping on his back. He wears boxer shorts, no top. The covers have been kicked off. We see the surprisingly large and still raw scar inscribed across his chest—the result of the emergency operation that saved his life.*

The intercom buzzer sounds in the next room. Again. Three, four times. Each ring is longer and more insistent than the one before it.

IZZY'*s eyelids flutter. He opens his eyes. Cut to:*

13. INT: DAY. IZZY'S APARTMENT. THE FRONT DOOR.

A minute later. IZZY, *wearing a bathrobe, opens the door. His ex-wife,* HANNAH, *is standing in the hall. She is an energetic, dark-haired woman in her mid-thirties.*

IZZY

(*Taken aback*) Oh. It's you.

(*Stepping past him into the apartment*) You don't pick up your phone, so I figured I'd pay you a visit.

Barely pausing, she marches off in the direction of the kitchen, leaving the frame. We hear the banging of cupboards, the sound of running water, a refrigerator door opening and closing, the rattling of pots and pans. IZZY shuts the front door, follows her to the threshold of the kitchen, and observes her from behind. For once he seems amused. Her energy seems to have lifted him temporarily out of the doldrums.

IZZY

You look nice in those pants.

HANNAH

(*Over her shoulder*) Don't get any ideas, chum. What's inside these pants is strictly off limits.

IZZY

Don't worry. It just brings back memories, that's all. That plump, protruding little ass of yours. For a year or two, it was the most interesting place in the world for me.

HANNAH

My ass and I are doing just fine without you, Izzy. You're not the only man who's ever admired it, you know.

IZZY

So I gathered. You don't get a tan like that hanging around the city. That new boyfriend of yours must be working out okay. (*Steps into the kitchen*) What is it? A house in the Hamptons, or something more exotic?

HANNAH

(*Busying herself with making coffee, pouring juice, popping bread into the toaster*) We'll get to him later. We have other things to talk about first.

IZZY

Like what?

HANNAH

Like you, dumbbell, that's what. I want to know what's happening to you.

IZZY

What for? I mean, you don't even *like* me.

HANNAH

You still don't know who I am, do you? After all these years, you still don't have a clue.

IZZY

Apparently not.

HANNAH

Once I give my heart to someone, it's forever. I might not want to live with you anymore, but that doesn't mean I don't care about you. (*Beat*) You're still a part of who I am, you jerk.

14. INT: DAY. IZZY'S APARTMENT. THE LIVING ROOM.

Half an hour later. IZZY and HANNAH are sitting at a small table in a corner of the living room, eating breakfast. The saxophone case is still on the floor— but in a different spot. Stereo equipment. Hundreds of records, tapes, and CDs. A few dozen books. Posters on the walls.

HANNAH

So what do you do with yourself, Izzy? How do you spend your time?

IZZY

The usual stuff. Breathing, eating, sleeping, trying to keep my head screwed on straight.

And you don't feel . . . lonely?

IZZY

Well, I read a lot of newspapers. That's one way of keeping in touch with your fellow human beings. You'd be amazed how much they can cram into one paper. (*Beat*) So many sad things, Hannah. It can really knock the stuffing out of you sometimes.

HANNAH

That's why I only read the comics.

IZZY

(*Ignoring her comment. Earnestly*) Most of it I can take. The fires, the earthquakes, the plane crashes. Even political horrors . . . wars . . . stuff like that. It's life, after all. It's what people do to each other, and you have to try to understand it.

HANNAH

You sound like you're seventeen years old.

IZZY

(*Still ignoring her*) But then, sometimes, you run across a little story on one of the back pages, and your heart just stops beating. A mother boils her baby in the Bronx. A man sets his girlfriend's daughter on fire in Brooklyn. I mean, it's so easy to turn life into garbage, isn't it?

HANNAH

It's not your life, Izzy. You can't go around tearing yourself apart over every rotten thing that happens.

IZZY

I don't. At least I don't make a big point of it. But these people live in the same city I do. I'd like to forget it, but sometimes I just can't.

HANNAH

Toughen up, sport. Put the chip back on your goddamn shoulder.

IZZY

(*Beat. Reflects*) I'm not the same person I used to be.

HANNAH

(*Studying him*) Don't change too much, okay? (*Beat*) You don't have to be miserable if you don't want to.

IZZY

I'm not miserable. (*Beat*) As a matter of fact, I think I'm doing okay.

HANNAH

(*Smiles*) Good. Then you're well enough to come over for dinner next week and meet Philip.

IZZY

So that's his name, huh?

HANNAH

Philip Kleinman. He's a movie producer.

IZZY

Never heard of him.

HANNAH

Big surprise. When was the last time you went to the movies, Iz?

IZZY

About twelve years ago.

HANNAH

Not since Gene Kelly retired, huh?

IZZY

Now that he's dead, I'll probably never go to the movies again.

HANNAH

(*Changing the subject*) You're going to like him. I guarantee it.

IZZY

And if I don't?

HANNAH

Then you can sit there and eat your food.

IZZY

And watch you be happy.

HANNAH

That's right. And see with your own eyes that I've finally gotten you out of my system.

15. INT: NIGHT. PHILIP KLEINMAN'S APARTMENT. TRIBECA.

We see HANNAH from behind, opening the front door. IZZY has arrived for the dinner party.

IZZY

(*Awkward*) Hi.

HANNAH

(*Ironical*) Excuse me if I'm in shock. (IZZY *steps into the apartment*) I didn't think you'd come.

IZZY

You invited me, remember?

SONIA, KLEINMAN's ten-year-old daughter, wanders into the entrance hall.

SONIA

(*To* IZZY) Hi.

IZZY

Hi.

HANNAH

(*To* IZZY) This is Sonia, Philip's daughter.

SONIA

(*Hesitates briefly*) Are you Izzy Maurer?

IZZY

Well, I used to be.

SONIA

Who are you now?

IZZY

(*Smiles*) I don't know. Maybe nobody.

SONIA

Well, nice to meet you, Mr. Nobody. (*Starts walking down the hallway to her room. Stops. Over her shoulder*) See you around.

HANNAH

(*Taking* IZZY *by the arm and steering him toward the living room*) There's been a slight change in plans. Philip's working on a project with Catherine Moore, and she's in New York for a few days, so we invited her to dinner too.

IZZY

The actress?

HANNAH

Former actress. She's a director now. She hasn't acted in ten or fifteen years.

IZZY

Catherine Moore. (*Beat. Remembering*) I used to have a crush on her.

Cut to:

The dining room. Time has passed. PHILIP KLEINMAN, *a lively man in his forties, and* CATHERINE MOORE, *an English woman in her late fifties, are sitting at the table with* IZZY *and* HANNAH. *They are coming to the end of the meal.*

IZZY

(*To* CATHERINE) So what made you give up acting?

CATHERINE

Vanity, Mr. Maurer. Beauty fades. The flesh gives out. You lose interest in being someone else's idea about who you are. I didn't want to be invented by other people anymore.

IZZY

So now you invent yourself.

CATHERINE

Exactly. I'm the one who controls the images.

IZZY

But no one sees you.

CATHERINE

(*Laughs*) So much the better. (*Beat*) They see what I think.

PHILIP

What they'll be seeing next is a new version of *Pandora's Box*. After a thousand bends in the road, we finally have a deal in place. (*Beat*) All we need is someone to play Lulu.

IZZY

Who's Lulu?

HANNAH

(*A little exasperated*) Come on, Maurer. Enough with the jokes already.

IZZY

No, I'm serious. Who's Lulu?

HANNAH

Lulu. As in Louise Brooks. As in Frank Wedekind. As in the opera by Alban Berg.

IZZY

Oh, that Lulu. Yeah. It rings a faint bell.

PHILIP

The girl who eats men for breakfast. You know, the one who's done in by Jack the Ripper.

CATHERINE

(*Turning to* PHILIP; *referring to a previous conversation*) You see what I mean, Philip? It's not at all obvious. People don't remember anything.

HANNAH

Don't worry, Catherine. It's not people, it's Izzy. Talk to him about anything but music and he's like a little kid.

PHILIP

(*Spotting* SONIA *enter the room*) Speaking of kids . . . (*Beat, as* SONIA *approaches the table*) Hi, sweetheart.

SONIA gives a little wave to the company, then stops by CATHERINE, *whose chair is closest to the door.* CATHERINE *studies* SONIA *for a moment, then reaches out and strokes her face gently with her hand. She is clearly taken with the girl's youth and loveliness.* SONIA *smiles and puts her hand on* CATHER-INE's *shoulder.*

CATHERINE

(*To* SONIA) And so, my little beauty, are you going to be an actress when you grow up?

SONIA

No. I'm going to be a writer. Books are better than movies, don't you think? You see the pictures in your head.

PHILIP

Ten years old, and she has an opinion about everything.

HANNAH

(*To* SONIA) You getting tired?

SONIA

Yeah. I came out to say good night.

HANNAH

Do you want me to tuck you in?

SONIA

Is that okay?

HANNAH

(*To* PHILIP) You don't mind, do you?

PHILIP

Mind? Why should I mind?

HANNAH

(*Smiles. Gets up from her chair*) Okay. I'll be back in a few minutes.

CATHERINE

Is it all right if I go, too?

SONIA

(*Suddenly playful. Goes into a limp-wristed pose and puts on a broad New York accent*) Of cawse, dawling. I'd be chawmed.

SONIA *leaves the room with a mincing, exaggerated feminine walk.* CATHERINE *and* HANNAH *follow—both imitating her. The two women laugh. A wide shot of the three leaving the room.*

When they are gone, PHILIP *takes two large cigars out of his pocket and extends one to* IZZY.

IZZY

No, thanks.

PHILIP

(*Lighting his own cigar. Thoughtful, studying* IZZY *carefully*) Do you mind if I ask you a question?

IZZY

(*Uncertain about what* PHILIP *is driving at*) A question? Sure. Ask any question you want.

PHILIP

You don't have to answer if you don't want to. But something happened to me a couple of weeks ago, and I'm still trying to figure out if I did the right thing or not.

IZZY

You want to know what I would have done in your place?

PHILIP

Right. If you had been me, how would you have acted. (*Puffs on his cigar*) I was on a plane to London—going to see Catherine, as a matter of fact. Just as we go into our descent, I decide I have to go to the toilet. I go down the aisle, but the door is locked, so I stand there shooting the breeze with one of the stewardesses. (*Puffs on his cigar*) Finally, the door opens and out steps this good-looking girl. Very pretty, maybe twenty-four or twenty-five. She gives me an odd little look—something between a smile and a frown—and then she edges past me and I go into the bathroom. (*Puffs on his cigar*) The toilet seat and the cover are both down, and sitting on the cover is a huge turd. (*Puffs again*) I have no idea what to do. This good-looking girl has dumped her business all over the toilet seat cover, and I can't lift the thing to do *my* business without facing . . . uh . . . certain unpleasant problems. (*Puffs again*) If I complain to the stewardess, she'll think I did it. We've just had this friendly conversation, and I don't want her to think I'm that kind of person. (*Gesturing with the cigar*) Besides, there isn't much time. We're going to land in about seven minutes, and the only thing I'm really interested in is emptying my bowels and getting back to my seat. (*Puffs again*) That's the situation. Now tell me what you would have done if you'd been me.

IZZY

(*Thoughtful*) I don't know. (*Beat*) I would have complained, I guess, but I'm not sure. (*Beat*) What did you do?

PHILIP

I took out some paper towels and cleaned up the mess.

IZZY

(*Impressed*) Incredible.

PHILIP

Yeah. Incredibly disgusting.

IZZY

(*Thinking it over*) I think it was a noble thing. You didn't complain. You spared the girl's feelings. You took responsibility for her when you didn't have to. (*Beat*) I don't think I've ever done anything that generous. (*Beat*) You did an admirable thing.

PHILIP

Maybe, maybe not. I'm still not sure. Maybe I was just being a coward. You know, trying to avoid a scene.

IZZY

Maybe. But I still think you acted like a mensch.

SUDDENLY: a loud blast of rock 'n' roll music is heard from the other end of the apartment. "Big Girls Don't Cry" is playing at full volume. Cut to:

SONIA's room. SONIA, HANNAH, and CATHERINE are dancing to the song and singing the words: laughing, having a great time together. After a moment, PHILIP and IZZY appear in the doorway and watch. HANNAH and CATHERINE wave to them. SONIA blows a kiss. The dancing continues.

16. EXT: NIGHT. STREET MONTAGE.

We see IZZY leaving PHILIP KLEINMAN's building. He heads north. Walking is still difficult for him, but his coordination and stamina have improved since his outing in scene 10.

It is after eleven o'clock. An autumn night in New York. The streets are crowded with pedestrians, traffic. Sound distortions: snatches of conversations, the whoosh of passing rollerblades, the rattling of manhole covers as trucks pass over them—as if IZZY has entered a state of intense alertness, a zone of rare perceptual sensitivity.

He winds up somewhere in the westernmost part of lower Manhattan, walking along empty streets lined with old warehouses and converted loft buildings.

Not another soul is in sight. It has become so still that IZZY has become aware of the sound of his own footsteps. They resonate against the pavement. At one point, he stops to listen—suddenly afraid that someone might be following him. He looks around. There is no one. He has been making the sound himself.

Walking west, a block from the Hudson River. Twenty or thirty feet ahead, lit by a glowing street lamp, IZZY catches a glimpse of a man. The man is lying on the ground, his head on the sidewalk and his feet in the gutter—sprawled out like a drunk.

IZZY continues walking, but more slowly now, sensing that something might be wrong. Closer: we can see that the man is dressed in a pinstriped business suit, that he is wearing a white shirt and a tie. Hardly the clothing of a drunk or a man who sleeps in the streets. His neatly polished shoes gleam in the light of the lamp.

Closer still. We hear the mounting panic in IZZY's breath, the shudderings of fear that pass through his body. IZZY approaches.

The man is dead. He has been shot through the middle of his forehead, and his eyes stare vacantly upward, reflecting the light of the street lamp.

IZZY lowers himself to the ground, crouches over the body, and looks at the dead man's face. A moment of horror. The man is thirty-five or forty. Short, sandy hair; a squarish, All-American face. IZZY can't take his eyes off the bullet hole in the middle of his forehead. The camera moves in on the bloody circle, that death hole that stares back like a third eye. Extreme close-up. IZZY feels that he is drowning in it, sinking straight into the center of the dead man's brain.

The man isn't a stranger so much as another version of himself. It is as if IZZY is looking at his own death, the death that almost was.

Finally, he can't take it anymore. He turns away from the dead man, pivoting so abruptly on the balls of his feet that he falls down. As he hits the ground, a

terrible noise escapes from his lungs. A breath, an immense outrush of breath—
as if he has been too scared to breathe.

He tries to stand up but is still so winded that he stumbles and falls again. He
crawls off on all fours, moving away from the gutter toward the shadow of the
nearest building. He collapses again, landing on top of a briefcase, which is
lying on the sidewalk. No doubt it belongs to the dead man.

Not even aware of what he is doing, IZZY grabs hold of the briefcase and
clutches it to his chest. He slowly climbs to his feet. Without turning back to
look at the dead man, he staggers off into the darkness.

17. INT: NIGHT. IZZY'S APARTMENT. THE LIVING ROOM.

IZZY is sitting at the table, drinking a glass of bourbon. The bottle is beside
him. In front of him: the briefcase. He studies it for a long time, reluctant to
open it, yet unable to turn his eyes away.

At last: he undoes the latch. He reaches his hand inside. One by one, he pulls
out: a credit card receipt slip (slightly crumpled, as if it has been thrown into
the briefcase and forgotten); a paper napkin with a telephone number written
on it; a pale blue Tiffany box, sealed up with ample amounts of Scotch tape,
measuring about five inches along each side. He puts his hand back into the
briefcase and feels around for something more. Nothing. He turns the briefcase
upside down and shakes it. Nothing.

He examines the credit card slip. Insert shot. The name of the cardholder is
STANLEY MAR. The purchase was for a seventy-five-dollar necktie at Barney's
on 4-12-96.

Next, he examines the napkin. Insert shot: Scrawled in blurry ink from a felt-
tip pen, we read: 555-0192.

Then, and only then, the box. He tries to tear off the tape with his fingers. It
is stubborn, and it takes some time for him to remove it. Inside the box there

31

is another box—this one made of sturdy brown cardboard and taped even more securely than the first.

IZZY tries to tear off the tape with his fingers, but with no success. He gets up from the table and leaves the frame. The camera stays on the box. We hear noises from the kitchen. IZZY comes back into the frame holding a paring knife. He sits down at the table and slits open the tape with the knife. Inside the second box there is a third box. This one is black and shiny and quite small—about three inches along each side. IZZY slits the tape and removes the top. There are small strips of shredded newspaper inside—a nest of packing excelsior. Hidden inside the papers there is a small stone. It is an irregular lump of hard material approximately two to two-and-a-half inches in diameter. It easily fits inside IZZY's palm.

He puts the stone down on the table. Insert shot. The stone is a stone only in the loosest sense of the term. It clearly doesn't come from the ground, and it clearly isn't precious or beautiful or any of the other things one might have expected it to be. It looks like a clump of construction material that has fallen off a building: a jagged shard of cement studded with gravel and glittering fragments of glass or mica. It is a homely, forlorn thing, a bit of late-twentieth-century detritus.

Around the edges of the frame during the insert shot, we see some of the strips of the shredded newspapers. The papers are written in different languages: Russian, Chinese, Hebrew, Arabic. Sound: all through this shot, a vague murmuring of different voices can be heard, male and female alike, each one speaking a different language.

Nothing can be heard distinctly. Every now and then, a word emerges from the confusion, but only for the smallest flicker of a second.

Shot of IZZY, sitting at the table. The murmurs continue. He picks up the stone, puts it down again, and stares at it. He pours himself another drink. Takes a sip, puts the glass down on the table, and continues to look at the stone.

18. INT: NIGHT. IZZY'S APARTMENT.
THE BEDROOM/THE LIVING ROOM.

Later. IZZY, *dressed in a T-shirt and boxer shorts, enters the bedroom with the stone in his hand. He puts it down on the bedside table, climbs into bed, and turns out the light.*

Obscurity. We see IZZY *lying in bed, his eyes open, staring up at the ceiling. After a moment, a glowing blue light can be seen to his right, coming from the area of the bedside table. The source of the light, however, is not visible, since* IZZY's *body and head are blocking the view.*

After another moment, IZZY *notices the blue glow and is wrenched from his thoughts. He sits up suddenly, turns his head, and looks at the stone.*

Shot of the bedside table. The stone has utterly changed. It is smooth now, and all around it the air is bathed in a rich blue light.

IZZY *lets out a gasp of alarm. He quickly gets out of bed and rushes to the door. He flicks on the overhead light. Just like that, everything returns to normal. Shot of the bedside table. The stone looks as it did before. Shot of* IZZY. *He is breathing hard, panicked. He has no idea what is going on. He turns off the overhead light again. Obscurity. For a moment, nothing happens. Perhaps it was all a dream. Three, four beats. Then, just as* IZZY *is about to turn on the light again, the stone begins to glow once more. The same blue, the same mysterious light. After a few moments, the stone begins to levitate, rising three or four inches off the surface of the table. It hovers in the air for several moments, the blue light steadily intensifying. Beside himself with confusion and fear,* IZZY *turns on the light again. Shot of the bedside table. The stone as before. Cut to:*

The living room. IZZY *enters, turns on the light, and stumbles into the saxophone case. He kicks it aside. Goes to a chest of drawers. Opens the top right drawer and rummages inside, desperately sifting through various objects. Gives up; slams the drawer shut. Opens the top left drawer.*

Same desperate rummaging. Finds an old pack of cigarettes and a book of matches. Shakes a cigarette out and lights up. Takes a drag. It causes intense pain. He grabs hold of his chest and doubles over for a moment. Gradually pulls himself together. Sits down in the armchair. Cautiously takes another puff. The camera slowly moves in on IZZY's *face. His hand trembles as he brings the cigarette to his mouth.*

19. INT: DAY. IZZY'S APARTMENT. THE BEDROOM.

The next morning. IZZY, *looking haggard and unshaven, dressed in his bathrobe, stands by the bedside table, where the stone still sits from the previous night. Holding the napkin in his hand, he checks the telephone number that is written on it. He reaches for the telephone, then hesitates. He studies the phone for a moment. Reaches again, hesitates again. Takes a deep breath. Reaches a third time and picks up the receiver. Sound of the dial tone. Beat. Reluctant to dial, he looks at the number on the napkin again.*

Then, very quickly, he begins to dial the numbers . . .

20. INT: DAY. CELIA'S APARTMENT. THE KITCHEN.

The Katmandu CD is playing softly. CELIA *sits at the table wearing her bathrobe and drinking coffee. She has just woken up. The phone rings. She reaches for the phone (which is mounted on the wall) and lifts the receiver off the hook.*

CELIA

Hello . . . (*Listens*) Who? . . . You're kidding . . . Believe it or not, I'm listening to your record now . . . My name? How can you call me if you don't know my name? . . . Oh. I see . . . Celia Burns. (*Listens. Pronounces name more clearly*) Celia Burns. . . . All right. If it's that important . . . Okay . . . Two-fifty-eight West Twenty-fifth Street. Second floor . . . Fine. I'll see you then. (*Hangs up, completely perplexed*)

21. INT: DAY. CELIA'S APARTMENT. THE LIVING ROOM.

An hour later. CELIA, *dressed in casual clothes, opens the door.* IZZY *is standing in the doorway, holding a plastic bag in his left hand.*

IZZY

(*Hesitates*) Celia?

He studies her face. A brief moment of confusion—as if he recognizes her from somewhere.

CELIA

It *is* you. I recognize you from your picture. (IZZY *steps into the apartment and she shuts the door*) After I hung up, I thought someone might be playing a trick on me.

IZZY

No tricks. Just one question. Do you know a man named Stanley Mar?

35

CELIA

(*Puzzled*) Stanley Mar?

IZZY

M-A-R.

CELIA

I don't think so.

IZZY

(*Agitated*) Thirty-five, forty. Looks like a businessman, maybe a lawyer. Wears nice suits. Shops for his ties at Barney's.

Little by little, IZZY *is backing* CELIA *into the apartment. He is so upset, so consumed by his need to understand, that he scarcely takes any notice of her. She, on the other hand, is becoming a little frightened.*

CELIA

(*Backing away from him*) I don't know. Maybe. I had a drink with someone named Stanley about a year ago. He never told me his last name.

IZZY

(*Very agitated*) Maybe? What's this maybe. (*Takes the napkin with her address and phone number on it out of his pocket and thrusts it at her*) What's this? What the fuck is this?

CELIA

(*Studies the napkin*) This isn't my handwriting. (*Looks at* IZZY) How did you get this?

IZZY

He had it on him. And you're going to stand there and tell me you saw him only once?

CELIA

If it's the same Stanley we're talking about—yes. I work in a restaurant. I served him dinner one night, and he asked me out. I found him boring. All he talked about was money.

IZZY

(*Holding up the plastic bag. Adamant; nearly hitting her in the face with it*)
And what about this? I suppose you don't know anything about this,
either.

CELIA

(*Backing away; peeved; slowly gaining the upper hand*) I don't know what
you're talking about. (*Beat*) Look, I really like your music, and I'm
sorry about what happened to you, but you're acting like a crazy man.
If you don't calm down, I'm going to have to ask you to leave.

IZZY

(*Reaches into the bag, pulls out the black box, and holds it up*) You don't
understand.

*He puts the box on the coffee table, lifts the top off the box, and takes out the
stone. He shows it to her, holding it between two fingers.*

CELIA

(*Unimpressed; puzzled*) What is it?

IZZY

You tell me.

CELIA

(*Laughs*) Me?

IZZY

Mar was carrying two things with him. The napkin with your number on it—and this.

IZZY hands the stone to CELIA. She examines it.

CELIA

It doesn't look like anything. It's just . . . shit . . . a little piece of shit.
(*She hands it back to him*)

IZZY

I know. That's what it looks like, doesn't it? (*Beat*) Close the blinds.

CELIA

(*Thrown*) What?

IZZY

We have to make it dark in here. (*Puts the stone down on the coffee table, walks to a window, and pulls down the shade*) The darker the better.

CELIA

I don't like it when people order me around.

IZZY

(*Walks to another window; pulls down another shade*) Just humor me. I'm not going to hurt you. (*Pulling down another shade*) You don't mean anything to me—

CELIA

(*More and more peeved*) That's pretty obvious, isn't it?

IZZY

—I just have to show you this.

CELIA

(*Firm*) Five minutes. And then I want you out of here. Got it? I have better things to do than play games with you.

IZZY

(*Ignoring her; pulling down the last shade*) Okay. Now turn out the light.

CELIA *walks over to the light switch by the door. She flicks the switch, and the overhead light goes off. Obscurity.*

IZZY

Now watch.

A few beats. Nothing happens.

CELIA

(*Cynical*) I'm watching.

IZZY

(*Impatient*) Just wait. Give it a little time.

Close-up of the stone on the coffee table, barely visible in the obscurity. Little by little, it begins to glow, to become smooth, to emit the same blue light it did in IZZY's apartment.

A close-up of CELIA's face, bathed in the blue light. She is astonished, filled with wonder.

CELIA

Oh my God.

IZZY

You see?

CELIA

(*Awed*) It's beautiful. It's the most beautiful thing I've ever seen.

IZZY

And Mar never said anything to you about it?

CELIA

(*Transfixed by the light; not wanting to be interrupted*) Sshh!

CELIA begins walking toward the coffee table, approaching the stone, which is now hovering a few inches above the surface. The nearer she gets, the more intense and radiant the light becomes.

IZZY

(*Alarmed*) What are you doing?

CELIA

(*Standing near the stone; studying it; amazed*) Be quiet.

IZZY

Don't touch it!

CELIA

Why not?

IZZY

Because . . . because we don't know what it is.

CELIA

Don't be silly. Of course I'm going to touch it. (*Beat*) How could I not touch it?

She sits down on the sofa next to the coffee table, leans forward, and cups the glowing stone in her two hands. For a moment or two, she just sits there, absorbing the feel of it. Then, very slowly, she begins to smile. The stone seems to have produced some unexpected, happy effect. Another moment goes by, and she begins to laugh—softly, as if to herself, as if some daunting inner puzzle had suddenly been clarified. It is a laugh of knowledge, of understanding.

IZZY

What does it feel like?

CELIA

(*Not wanting to interrupt the experience—yet playful, teasing*) I'm not going to tell you. (*Beat, concentrating on the feel of the stone*) I don't share secrets with cowards.

IZZY

(*A little defensive*) I'm just not stupid, that's all.

CELIA

(*Looking up at him. Her face full of life, joy*) Oh, come on. Don't be afraid. It's the best thing. It really is. It's like nothing else.

She starts laughing again, swept away by the power of what is happening to her.

Reluctantly, IZZY walks over to the sofa and sits down beside her. He looks at CELIA suspiciously. After a moment, she reaches out with the stone, her arm fully extended. IZZY finally opens his hand, and she places the stone carefully in his palm. IZZY sits back and holds the stone in both hands. After a moment, he laughs nervously, surprised by what he is feeling.

CELIA

(*Studying him carefully*) It's amazing, isn't it?

IZZY

(*Sinking more deeply into the feeling*) Jesus . . . (*After a moment, hands the stone back to her. A long silence. Studies her intently*) You feel more alive, don't you?

CELIA

Yes. (*Beat. Thoughtful. Looking straight ahead*) More . . . connected.

IZZY

Connected to what?

CELIA

I don't know. (*Beat. Thinks. Still looking ahead*) To myself. To the table. To the floor. To the air in the room. To everything that's not me. (*Another beat*) To you.

Several more beats. She hands the stone back to IZZY. He holds it for a while before speaking. CELIA watches him.

IZZY

(*Looking ahead*) When I woke up this morning, I didn't know who you were. The way I'm feeling now, I think I could spend the rest of my life with you. I think I'd be willing to die for you.

CELIA

(*Growing upset*) Don't . . .

41

IZZY

I'm sorry. I'm just telling you the truth. (*Hands her the stone. Another beat*)

CELIA

Do you know what it means to die for someone? (*Long beat. Almost to herself*) It's not fair.

IZZY

Why not?

CELIA

Turn on the light. Please turn on the light.

A moment passes. IZZY gets up, walks to the nearest light switch, and turns it on. The room returns to normal. The blue stone returns to its original state. As IZZY walks around the room, opening the curtains and blinds, CELIA puts the stone back in the box. IZZY watches carefully.

IZZY

I think I should go now.

CELIA

I'm sorry.

IZZY

I'll come back tomorrow.

CELIA

Yes. Come back tomorrow.

He looks at her tenderly. She gives him a weak, confused smile. Hands him the box. He puts it in his pocket, touches her face with his hand. She kisses his hand gently.

Then he turns, walks to the door, and leaves the apartment. She continues to sit on the sofa. Watches the door close.

42

She leans back her head, arching her neck over the top of the sofa, puts her hands over her eyes. When she removes her hands, we see that she is blinking back tears. Close shot.

She stands up, fighting against her feelings, struggling not to break down. She begins tidying the living room—opening the curtains more, adjusting the blinds.

Suddenly, without coming to any apparent decision, she rushes across the room, opens the door, and leaves the apartment.

22. EXT: DAY. WEST TWENTY-FIFTH STREET.

IZZY is walking slowly down the street. Over his shoulder, we see CELIA running to catch up with him. She moves on past him, stops, and then turns to face him.

CELIA

(*Out of breath. A moment*) I have some shopping to do. I thought maybe you'd like to come with me.

IZZY

(*Studying her. A smile slowly forming*) Sounds good.

CELIA

Eggs, oranges, those kinds of things.

IZZY

You can't live if you don't eat, right?

23. INT: DAY. CELIA'S APARTMENT. THE BEDROOM.

Several hours later. IZZY and CELIA are in CELIA's bed, under the sheets. Daylight pours through the window. The stone is nowhere in sight. CELIA is awake, her head propped in one hand, watching IZZY, who is lying on his back. He has just opened his eyes.

CELIA

(*Smiling, tranquil, and yet totally puzzled*) I don't even know who you are.

IZZY

(*Reaching out and gently touching her face*) Yes you do. You know everything about me.

He sits up. We see the scar.

CELIA

(*Laughs*) Not really.

IZZY

But it doesn't matter, does it?

CELIA

No. As long as you don't get up and leave now, I don't suppose it does.

IZZY

(*Taking her in his arms; settling in*) You don't see me rushing to get out of here, do you?

CELIA

(*Her head on his chest, smiling. Beat*) Tell me, Izzy, are you an ocean or a river?

IZZY

What?

CELIA

It's a game I used to play with my sister. You have to answer.

IZZY

(*Catching on*) An ocean or a river. (*Thinks for a moment*) A river.

CELIA

Are you a . . . match . . . or a cigarette lighter?

IZZY

A match. Definitely a match.

CELIA

Are you a car . . . or a bicycle?

IZZY

A bicycle.

CELIA

Are you an owl or a hummingbird?

IZZY

Hmm. I used to be a hummingbird. But now I'm an owl.

CELIA

Are you sneakers or boots?

IZZY

That's not fair. You have to give me a chance now.

CELIA

(*Holding firm*) Sneakers or boots?

IZZY

Boots. (*Pulling her up so that he can see her face*) Now it's my turn.

CELIA

It's fun, isn't it? We used to do it for hours.

IZZY

(*Puts his fingers to his lips, as if to say no more talking*) All right now, concentrate. (*Beat. Entering a different register; very serious*) Are you a real person . . . or a spirit?

CELIA

(*Long beat; studying him; gradually becoming more emotional*) A real person.

IZZY

Do you understand what's happened, or are you in the dark like me?

CELIA

(*Trembling slightly*) In the dark.

IZZY

Are you in love . . . or just going along for the ride?

CELIA

(*With tears gathering in her eyes*) In love.

IZZY

Are you with the person you love . . . or not with the person you love?

CELIA

(*Begins to cry in earnest; overcome*) With the person. (*Close-up of her face. She repeats the line—almost inaudibly*) With the person.

24. EXT: DAY. CELIA'S BUILDING. THE ROOF.

IZZY and CELIA are sitting on a blanket on the roof. CELIA is dressed now; IZZY as before. The city sprawled out around them. We catch them in mid-conversation.

IZZY

There was a hole . . . right in the middle of his forehead . . . like a huge blind eye. I thought I was going to drown in it. Once I looked in there . . . I thought I'd never get out.

CELIA

(*Long beat. Absorbing what he has said. Touches him tenderly*) He must have been killed for the stone.

IZZY

Then why didn't they take it?

CELIA

(*Thoughtful*) Maybe something went wrong.

IZZY

I wish I could give it back.

CELIA

Back? Back to who?

IZZY

To the person who owns it. I don't know . . . to the place where it belongs.

CELIA

Do you know what it reminds me of?

IZZY

What?

CELIA

The Berlin Wall.

IZZY

Not big enough.

CELIA

Remember when the wall came down in eighty-nine? Little pieces of it were floating around all over the place. A friend of mine was given one in Germany. It looked exactly the same . . . exactly like the thing you found.

IZZY

A cruddy little chunk of cement.

CELIA

Just like that.

IZZY

So you're saying that Russian scientists planted some mysterious substance in the Berlin Wall?

CELIA

No. I'm just telling you what it reminds me of.

IZZY

I'll tell you what it reminds me of. A piece of some building you see on a New Jersey highway. You know, a bowling alley, or a warehouse . . . or maybe some fly-by-night topless bar.

CELIA

(*Amused*) Why not?

IZZY

(*Beat. More serious*) Celia?

CELIA

(*Taking a sip of her drink. The pleasure of hearing him say her name*) Say it again.

IZZY

Celia.

CELIA

I love hearing you say that. (*Beat*) Say it again.

IZZY

Celia.

CELIA

(*As if melting*) Yes?

IZZY

(*Smiling*) Are you happier on this roof . . . or happier downstairs in bed?

Cut to:

25. INT: DAY. CELIA'S APARTMENT. THE BEDROOM.

Same as scene 23. IZZY and CELIA are in bed. They have just finished making love. Light pours through the windows.

IZZY is lying on his back. CELIA is touching and examining his scar.

CELIA

It's a beautiful scar. Without this scar, you wouldn't be alive. Without this scar . . . you wouldn't be here with me now. . . . Do you understand? It's a good and precious thing . . . (*Her eyes drift over to the alarm clock on the bedside table. It's five-thirty. Sudden panic*) Oh, my God! I have to go to work. (*Jumps out of bed and begins getting dressed*)

IZZY

(*Still lying in bed*) Why don't you call in sick?

CELIA

(*Rushing around*) I can't. I really can't. I've earned twelve hundred dollars as an actress this year. If I didn't have this job, I wouldn't eat.

IZZY

I don't want to let you out of my sight.

CELIA

I'll be back by midnight. You can wait for me here.

IZZY

(*Thinking*) Maybe I could work with you.

CELIA

What do you mean?

IZZY

I don't know. Maybe they need another waiter or something.

CELIA

(*She laughs at the absurdity of the proposal*) But you're a musician.

IZZY

Not anymore. My job is to be with you. That's my work now.

CELIA sits down on the bed and takes hold of his hand. Moved by what he has said.

CELIA

Are you real . . . or did I make you up?

IZZY

(*Pursuing the question*) Well?

CELIA

We could talk to Pierre.

IZZY

Pierre? What is it, a French restaurant?

CELIA

Not really. It's sort of fake French. Just like Pierre. I think he's from the Bronx. (*Beat*) There might be an opening for a busboy.

IZZY

I'll wash dishes if I have to.

CELIA

(*Leaning over and kissing him*) You'd better get dressed, then.

IZZY

(*Climbing out of bed. Touching his face*) I should shave, don't you think? Don't want to make a bad impression.

CELIA

Don't worry. If Pierre doesn't hire you, I'll tell him I'm going to quit.

26. INT: NIGHT. CHEZ PIERRE.

Close-up of a glass. We see ice water being poured into it. The camera backs up to reveal IZZY, *dressed in a white jacket, working as a busboy at Chez Pierre. It is dinnertime, and the place is crowded. Hustle, bustle, colliding conversations. We see* PIERRE *behind the bar, serving drinks to customers who are waiting for tables. Across the room,* CELIA *is taking orders at a table for four. She looks up and sees* IZZY *clearing away dishes from a table. Their eyes meet; they exchange a warm, complicitous smile.* PIERRE, *in between at the bar, notices their secret communication. He appears to be none too pleased. The camera lingers on* PIERRE's *face for a moment. A blood-curdling scream is heard. Cut to:*

27. INT: NIGHT. CELIA'S APARTMENT. THE TV SCREEN/THE LIVING ROOM.

A close-up of CELIA's *face: an expression of absolute terror. She is screaming her lungs out. From behind, we see a man walking toward her, backing her into a corner. Pounding music. Her arm is raised, and a butcher knife gleams in his hand.* CELIA *has run out of space. She sinks to her knees in despair.*

The camera backs up. The scene has been playing on the TV set in CELIA's *living room.* IZZY *and* CELIA *are watching together on the sofa, eating ice cream out of a container. It is a video reel of samples of* CELIA's *work.*

CELIA

That was the first part I got. Three years ago—just after I came to New York. *Horror Machine VI.* You take what you can get, right? (*Watching screen. Her expression changes; brightens enthusiastically*) Oh— watch this. It's a little bit I did in *The Laughing Man.*

Cut to the screen. CELIA, *wearing an elegant 1920s dress, is in a restaurant, sitting at a table with a man in a tuxedo. Jaunty music. She looks radiant, beautiful. She studies the menu, looks up, smiles at the man. An instant later, a cream pie hits her in the face.*

CELIA (off)

Pow!

IZZY (off)

(*Laughs*) That's terrible.

The TV screen goes black for a few moments.

CELIA

Now for some pure corn.

Next clip. CELIA, *dressed in a nun's habit, is sitting beside a hospital bed. A ten-year-old girl is lying there with her eyes closed—on the point of death, perhaps already dead. A religious choir sings in the background. Hands clasped together,* CELIA *prays for the child, her voice filled with conviction and suffering.*

CELIA ON SCREEN

. . . Yea though I walk through the valley of the shadow of death, I will fear no evil, for thou art with me . . .

The screen suddenly goes silent. We see the word MUTE *in the upper left-hand corner.*

CELIA *(off)*

You don't want to hear this.

IZZY *(off)*

Yes I do.

CELIA

It's awful.

IZZY

No it's not.

The MUTE *sign disappears.*

Surely goodness and mercy shall follow me all the days of my life, and I shall dwell in the house of the Lord forever.

After the clip ends, the screen goes black for a few moments, as before.

CELIA

This is something I did last year.

Next clip. CELIA, *wearing a blond wig, is sitting at a bar, smoking a cigarette and nursing a drink in front of her. She is clearly a prostitute.*

After a moment, a MAN *appears and sits down beside her. Sultry music plays in the background.*

IZZY

Hey, that's Lou Reed.

CELIA

No it's not. It just looks like him.

MAN ON SCREEN

Hi, Sweetheart.

CELIA ignores him, goes on smoking her cigarette.

MAN ON SCREEN *(cont'd)*

Looking for some fun?

CELIA ON SCREEN

(Cynical) Fun? What's your idea of fun, big guy?

MAN ON SCREEN

I don't know. You tell me.

CELIA ON SCREEN

(*Long beat, deciding whether or not to answer him*) It'll cost you fifty bucks to get me off this stool. You want me to walk through that door with you (*gestures with her head to the front door*), it'll cost you another fifty bucks. The motel charges seventy-five, and my rates start at a hundred and twenty per half hour. That's with my clothes on. You want me to take them off, it's another fifty. (*Beat*) Still interested?

MAN ON SCREEN

Yeah, I'm interested.

CELIA ON SCREEN

(*Sighs*) All right, be a good boy and go outside and wait for me. I want to finish my drink.

The MAN *hesitates for a second, then gets up and leaves.* CELIA *takes a drag of her cigarette and stares ahead, then lifts the glass to her lips. The screen goes black for a few moments, as before.*

IZZY

Jesus, you're one tough cookie.

CELIA

Scary, isn't it? (*Beat*) I really liked doing that scene. (*Clicks off the TV with the remote control*) Not much to show for myself so far.

IZZY

Nun . . . whore . . . murder victim . . . and a pie in the face. I'd say you're off to a good start.

CELIA

Movies are tough. I've always had better luck with plays. (*Beat*) I got an agent two months ago. She's the one who put together this tape.

IZZY

Has it helped?

CELIA

Yes and no. I've had more auditions—but no work yet. (*Beat*) I have another audition Monday afternoon.

IZZY

What's the part?

CELIA

Lulu. There's going to be a new version of *Pandora's Box*.

IZZY

(*Stunned*) You're kidding.

CELIA

(*Not understanding*) No, it's really happening. They're looking for someone completely unknown. (*With self-deprecation*) So maybe I have a chance. (*Beat*) I'd love to do that part. It's one of the best roles ever written for a woman.

IZZY

I know the people making that movie. Catherine Moore—she's the director, right? And Philip Kleinman's the producer.

CELIA

You know them?

IZZY

(*Enthusiastic*) Know them? I just had dinner with them a few days ago. I'll call them up, put in a word for you . . . get the ball rolling. (*Laughs. Claps his hands, rubs them together*) I'm going to get you that part, Celia. You watch. With me around, you don't need an agent.

28. EXT: DAY. NEW YORK STREET CORNER. CORNER OF PRINCE AND LAFAYETTE.

IZZY is talking to someone from a pay phone on the corner, watching the entrance of the building at 225 Lafayette Street.

IZZY

I just wanted to thank you, Hannah. You've been great. (*Listens*)

Shot of CELIA *leaving the building.*

IZZY

There she is now. I'll catch you later. (*Hangs up*)

CELIA *is standing in front of the door, looking around.*

IZZY *(still not at normal speed, but less hobbled by his injuries than before) rushes into the frame, puts his arm around* CELIA'S *shoulder, and kisses her on the cheek.*

IZZY

How did it go?

(*Looking uncertain*) I don't know.

They begin walking down the street.

CELIA (*cont'd*)

I don't think I was very good.

They walk for a moment in silence

CELIA (*cont'd*)

But it was a good experience. I got to talk to Catherine Moore, anyway. She's fantastic. An incredible woman.

The camera pulls back. We see CELIA *and* IZZY *walking down the street together from behind. We no longer hear what they are saying.*

29. INT: NIGHT. CHEZ PIERRE.

Another crowded dinner hour at the restaurant. IZZY *goes about his job, pouring ice water into glasses at various tables. He glances up and sees* CELIA *taking orders at a table occupied by three businessmen in their thirties. This time, the bar is manned by someone other than Pierre—who is off in the kitchen.*

Closer shot of CELIA *with the three men. They all appear to be rather drunk. Each one studies* CELIA *with lust in his eyes, looking her up and down. She stands there with her order pad, pretending not to notice.*

FIRST MAN

You wouldn't be free later tonight, would you?

CELIA

(*Matter-of-factly*) Sorry, I'm busy. (*Beat*) Have you decided on your orders?

SECOND MAN

She's just playing hard-to-get.

THIRD MAN

We'd be happy to . . . uh . . . make it worth your while.

CELIA

The duck is very good tonight. The chef is recommending it.

FIRST MAN

Fuck the duck. (*Laughs at his own witless joke*) I'm interested in other kinds of meat.

Reaches out and pats CELIA *on the behind. She swats his hand away.*

Shot of IZZY. *He has seen what has just happened. He puts down the pitcher of ice water on the table he is serving and rushes over to the table with the three men.*

IZZY

(*Addressing the* FIRST MAN. *Angry*) Hey, stupid. Keep your hands to yourself.

CELIA

It's all right, Izzy. I can handle it.

FIRST MAN

(*To* IZZY) Mind your own business, (*spitting out the next two syllables with contempt*) bus-boy.

SECOND MAN

Yeah. Go and clear away some dirty dishes.

IZZY

(*To* FIRST MAN) This is my business, asshole.

CELIA

(*Growing alarmed. Trying to push* IZZY *away*) It's nothing. Believe me, it's nothing.

(*Boiling into a rage*) Nothing? This schmuck starts feeling you up, and you call it nothing?

He pushes CELIA *aside. Goes after the* FIRST MAN *and grabs him violently by the lapels. Pain shoots through his left hand. He drops his left arm but continues holding on with his right. With one hand, he pulls the* FIRST MAN *out of his chair.*

IZZY

Come on, wise guy—do it again! I dare you. Do it again!

IZZY *throws the* FIRST MAN *backwards—straight into a nearby table. Clattering plates, silverware, overturned wine glasses. A woman shrieks. A general commotion breaks out in the restaurant.* IZZY *goes after the* FIRST MAN *again. The* SECOND MAN *and the* THIRD MAN *get up from their seats and go after* IZZY. PIERRE *comes running from the kitchen. He is beside himself with fury.*

PIERRE

Stop it! Stop it!

He pushes aside the SECOND MAN *and* THIRD MAN, *then wraps his arms around* IZZY *in a powerful bear hug from behind—just as* IZZY *is about to punch the* FIRST MAN *in the face.*

PIERRE

(*To* IZZY) How dare you! How dare you!

Wrestling him away from the others, he pushes IZZY *toward the bar, then— releasing him—throws him roughly against it.* IZZY *bangs his back against the panel and falls to the ground. A sense of* IZZY's *weakness, of the physical toll this outburst has caused him.*

PIERRE

Are you trying to ruin this business! Is that what you want—to destroy me!

IZZY *slowly climbs to his feet.* PIERRE *grabs him again.*

PIERRE

I'll kill you, you son-of-a-bitch! Do you hear me! I'll kill you!

CELIA tries to pull PIERRE away from IZZY.

PIERRE

(*Shrugging her off*) I never should have hired this maniac. I never should have let you talk me into it.

Suddenly returns to his senses a little bit. Sees the THREE MEN and other CUSTOMERS starting to leave the restaurant. In gracious, accommodating tones.

PIERRE

Please, everyone, please go back to your seats. I'm sorry for the disturbance. (*Chasing after the THREE MEN*) Please, gentlemen, please return to your table. Dinner is on the house tonight.

The departing customers return. BUSBOYS, WAITERS, *and* WAITRESSES *begin clearing up the mess caused by the fight.* PIERRE *turns his attention back to* IZZY, *who is still standing by the bar. With calm and bitter determination.*

PIERRE

You—I want out of my sight. Get your things and leave. You're fired.

CELIA

Pierre, please . . . it won't happen again.

PIERRE

(*Ignoring her appeal*) You're damned right it won't. If he ever sets foot in my place again, I'll tear him apart.

CELIA

(*Standing firm; defending* IZZY) If he goes, I go.

PIERRE

Then go. I don't care. You brought this bum in, you can take him out.

CELIA

(*Upset. To* PIERRE) You don't know what you're saying . . .

PIERRE

(*To* CELIA) I used to be the only friend you had. . . . (*Looks at* IZZY; *shakes his head*) Bad move, Celia. Very bad move.

PIERRE *turns to leave, stops, is about to address one last line to her but thinks better of it and walks away.*

30. EXT: NIGHT. MANHATTAN STREETS.

A few minutes later. CELIA *and* IZZY *are walking along slowly, side by side.* CELIA *is very agitated.*

CELIA

(*On the point of tears*) How could you do that? Do you know how much I need that job? Two-and-a-half years I've been working there—and in one night you ruin everything.

IZZY

(*Not defending himself. Contrite, ashamed*) I'm sorry. That's how I used to be. All crazy and wild. I'm sorry. I don't want to be that person anymore. I swear to you, I'll never act that way again.

31. INT: NIGHT. CELIA'S APARTMENT.

CELIA and IZZY enter the apartment in silence. They are both out of sorts, grumpy, not finished with their quarrel. IZZY heads straight for the bathroom and bangs the door shut. CELIA goes into the bedroom. A light is flashing on the answering machine. She sits down on the bed and plays the message.

WOMAN'S VOICE

Celia, this is Maggie. I've just had two calls. One from Philip Kleinman and one from Catherine Moore—and you've got the part. You're the one they want. It's fantastic. Call me tomorrow morning, and I'll fill you in on the details. Congratulations, darling. I'm just over the moon for you.

CELIA is stunned. She sits on the bed without moving. At that moment, IZZY walks into the bedroom. She looks up and smiles at him, a strange expression on her face.

IZZY

Are you all right?

CELIA

I got the part. I'm Lulu.

32. INT: DAY. ODEON RESTAURANT.

A celebratory Sunday brunch. Five people are present, sitting at a round table: IZZY, CELIA, PHILIP KLEINMAN, HANNAH, and CATHERINE MOORE. Begin with a close shot of IZZY's face. He is happy, enjoying himself, pleased to have played such an important part in getting CELIA the role. To one side of him, PHILIP and HANNAH are talking to each other; to the other side, CELIA *and* CATHERINE *are engrossed in conversation.* IZZY *alone says nothing, listening to both pairs of speakers at once, turning his attention now to one pair, now to the other. We hear bits of what each pair is saying.*

PHILIP *and* HANNAH *are studying* CELIA *across the table.* IZZY *watches them as they watch her. After a moment, he abruptly turns his attention to* CELIA *and* CATHERINE.

CATHERINE

"We are all lost creatures," he said. "It is only when we admit this that we have a chance of finding ourselves."

CELIA

But Lulu doesn't admit anything. She doesn't *know* anything. She just is.

CATHERINE

Wedekind said that Lulu isn't a real character, that she's an embodiment of primitive sexuality . . . and whatever evil she causes comes about by accident—because she's passive, because she plays a purely passive role.

CELIA

(*Thinks again*) No . . . I don't agree. She's impulsive, but she's not a destroyer. . . . She doesn't care what people think of her. That's what gives her her power. She has no pretensions. She doesn't play by the same rules as everyone else.

CATHERINE

(*Testing her*) But Wedekind wrote the play. He created her.

CELIA

It doesn't matter. He was wrong.

CATHERINE

(*Smiles. As if to herself*) We'll see.

Cut back to HANNAH.

HANNAH

So, Izzy, I hear you're going to be hanging around Dublin with us.

IZZY

(*Jolted from his thoughts*) Huh?

CELIA

(*To* HANNAH) He'll be getting there a few days after I do.

IZZY

(*To* HANNAH) Yeah. I'm getting rid of my apartment . . . putting my things in storage. When the movie's over, Celia and I are going to look for a new place together.

HANNAH

(*Happy for them, but with a slight pang*) Sounds cozy.

CELIA

(*Sure of herself*) It will be.

Shot from under the table. We see CELIA's *hand reach out and begin to touch* IZZY's *thigh. He takes hold of her hand in his.*

PHILIP (*off*)

Catherine, did you talk to Max about using bigger speakers for the rock 'n' roll scene?

CATHERINE (*off*)

He's taking care of it. I still haven't figured out how we'll light it, though.

PHILIP

Well, you'll be there the day after tomorrow. You can discuss it with George at the soundstage.

Cut to close-up of CELIA, *whispering into* IZZY's *ear.*

CELIA

Meet me downstairs. I have to talk to you.

IZZY looks around at the others, then stands up.

IZZY

(*To no one in particular*) Excuse me. I'll be back in a minute.

The camera follows IZZY as he walks away from the table and heads for the stairs. Just as he is about to go down, he turns around for a parting glance at CELIA. Cut to:

IZZY'S POV: Long shot of CELIA sitting at the table with the others.

She turns surreptitiously toward IZZY, meets his gaze, and smiles.

33. INT: DAY. ODEON RESTAURANT. DOWNSTAIRS.

An open area with a sofa, a couple of chairs, a potted plant, a pay telephone, the rest room doors. IZZY is standing there, waiting.

A moment later, he sees CELIA *coming quickly down the stairs. She rushes straight into his arms and begins kissing him—passionately, tenderly, not caring who sees her.*

34. INT: DAY. WEST TWENTY-FIFTH STREET. OUTSIDE CELIA'S BUILDING.

A black town car is parked in front of CELIA'S *door. The driver sits behind the wheel, waiting.*

35. INT: DAY. CELIA'S APARTMENT.

IZZY

(*Looking through the window*) The car is here.

CELIA'S *packed bags are in front of the door. She walks over to the window and looks down at the street with* IZZY.

CELIA

I wish you were going with me now.

IZZY

It's better this way. You can settle in, and I'll take care of things here. It's just a few days.

CELIA

(*Hugging him*) I don't want to let you out of my sight. I need you with me.

IZZY

(*Wrapping his arms around her*) You're going to knock their socks off.

CELIA

(*She smiles but is not really comforted. Putting her head against his chest*) I love you, Izzy.

IZZY

(*Holding her tight*) What did I do to deserve you? (*Beat*) You're my angel, Celia. My miracle. My whole life. (*Several beats. Disengages his right arm from her and reaches into his pocket. Pulls out the little black box and gives it to her*) Here, take this. Maybe it will help.

CELIA

(*Taking the box with one hand, still holding him closely with the other*) What for?

IZZY

Every time you look at it, you'll think about me.

CELIA

And what about you? Aren't you going to think about me?

IZZY

I don't need the stone for that. I'll be thinking about you every minute.

36. EXT: DAY. WEST TWENTY-FIFTH STREET. OUTSIDE CELIA'S BUILDING.

IZZY *slams the back door of the car shut. The car pulls away.* IZZY *stands there and watches. After a moment,* CELIA *sticks her head out the window and looks back at him. She blows him a kiss. The car continues to move down the street. She blows another kiss.*

Close-up of IZZY's *face, the palm of his right hand open beside it in a farewell gesture. A couple of beats. He lets his hand drop. A sense of loneliness, isolation.*

37. EXT: DAY. MANHATTAN STREET.

IZZY *walks downtown, heading toward his apartment in the Village.*

38. EXT: DAY. PERRY STREET. OUTSIDE IZZY'S BUILDING.

IZZY approaches the building, walks up the front steps, opens the door, and goes inside.

39. INT: DAY. IZZY'S APARTMENT.

IZZY steps into the apartment, shuts the door (without locking it), and turns on the light. He looks around for a few seconds, trying to get his bearings. He hasn't been there in weeks, and it's as if he has walked in on a stranger's life.

Suddenly, as if out of nowhere, three THUGS (one Russian, one German, one Chinese) burst into the apartment. Before IZZY can say a word, the GERMAN THUG grabs him from behind and the CHINESE THUG punches him in the stomach. IZZY doubles over in pain.

RUSSIAN THUG

(*Heavy accent*) You're a slippery fellow, Mr. Maurer. Don't you like your apartment anymore?

IZZY

(*Gasping for breath, still aching from the punch*) Who are you? . . . What do you want?

RUSSIAN THUG

No, Mr. Maurer, who are *you,* and what do *you* want? What gives you the right to meddle in our business?

CHINESE THUG

(*Heavy accent. To the* RUSSIAN) Again, boss?

RUSSIAN THUG

Absolutely.

The CHINESE THUG punches him again. IZZY falls down. The GERMAN THUG kicks him in the back. IZZY howls.

GERMAN THUG

(*Heavy accent*) Who are you working for, and why did you kill Stanley Mar?

IZZY

(*Sprawled out, struggling against the pain. Gets up on one knee*) I didn't kill him.

RUSSIAN THUG

It's too late for lies, my friend.

The GERMAN THUG *grabs hold of* IZZY *and pulls him to his feet.* IZZY *totters for a moment. Then the* CHINESE THUG *punches him in the face, and* IZZY *falls down again.*

40. EXT. DAY: DUBLIN AIRPORT.

Morning. An Aer Lingus plane lands on the runway.

41. INT: NIGHT. A ROOM SOMEWHERE.

IZZY, *badly beaten, wakes up to find himself lying on a cement floor. He seems to be in a basement room somewhere. Gray cinder-block walls, utterly bare and empty. A thick metal door. One small window at the top of one wall. Opaque, wire-reinforced glass. Dimness.* IZZY *rolls over and groans, still barely conscious.*

42. INT: DAY. IZZY'S APARTMENT.

The telephone is ringing in the living room of IZZY'S *apartment. The place is in turmoil: overturned furniture, books and records scattered across the floor, torn clothes. The camera slowly pans the room. The phone stops ringing and* IZZY'S *voice comes on.*

IZZY'S VOICE

Leave a message, and I'll get back to you.

After the beep, we hear:

71

Izzy—I've missed you again. I'll be in tonight, so you can call me when you get back. Everything is fine here, but I miss you so much, I can't wait to see you. Just three more days. *Just!* (*Laughs*) It feels like forever. I love you, Izzy. I kiss you. I send you a thousand hugs.

Cut to:

43. INT: NIGHT. DUBLIN. CELIA'S HOTEL ROOM.

CELIA *hangs up the phone. She is sitting beside a table. In front of her we see the little black box. She removes the lid, takes out the stone, and holds it in her palm—studying it carefully.*

44. INT: DAY. THE ROOM.

IZZY *wakes up in the bare, mysterious room. Dull light slants through the window. The bruises on* IZZY's *face have healed somewhat—suggesting that he has been there for several days.*

Once he returns to consciousness, he notices a box of crackers near the door. It has apparently been some time since he has eaten.

IZZY *crawls toward the door, takes hold of the crackers, and greedily rips open the box.*

He eats a cracker, chewing hard, desperate to satisfy his hunger. Then another cracker; then another—shoving them into his mouth like an animal. His cheeks fill up. The difficulty of swallowing.

He stops. Sorrow and fear overwhelm him. Struggling to rein in his emotions and stay calm, he begins to break down and cry. A series of choked-off, broken sobs. Little bits of cracker powder fly out of his mouth as the air leaves his lungs.

There is, of course, no water anywhere.

45. EXT: DAY. DUBLIN. ST. STEPHEN'S GREEN.

Sunday afternoon. CELIA *and* HANNAH *are strolling through the park. It is a bright tranquil day, and numerous other people are roaming about: young couples, families, children. The contrast between this setting and the atmosphere of the room in the previous scene should be made as stark as possible. An emphasis on the beauty of the surroundings, nature as opposed to the harshness of* IZZY's *cell. Green grass, trees, flowers, shrubs, sparrows, ducks bobbing on the surface of the pond.*

HANNAH

When will he be here?

CELIA

The day after tomorrow.

HANNAH

How does he sound?

CELIA

I don't know.

HANNAH

You don't know?

CELIA

He hasn't called. And I haven't been able to reach him.

HANNAH

Well, you know Izzy. Just when you think you know what he's going to do, he turns around and does something else.

CELIA

I'm starting to get worried.

HANNAH

He has a plane ticket, doesn't he? And an up-to-date passport?

CELIA

Yes.

HANNAH

Then don't worry. He'll be on that plane. I've seen how he looks at you—and believe me, there's no way he's not going to show up.

The camera cuts away to a young couple kissing under a tree, a toddler running across the grass, a bird hopping from a branch and taking off into the air.

CELIA

The funny thing is, I wouldn't be here if I hadn't met Izzy. He's the one who got me the part.

HANNAH

Not really. He made the phone call, but you got yourself the part.

CELIA

(*Thoughtful; struggling to express herself*) But it's all connected. I'm Lulu because Izzy loves me. Doing this role is part of our story together. I'm convinced of that.

HANNAH

But that's good, no?

CELIA

Yes, it's good. But Lulu scares me. She's a monster, really.

HANNAH

It's a tough role. I mean, Pandora opens the box, and all the evils of the world come flying out. (*Beat*) What I want to know is, who decided that Pandora is a woman?

CELIA

(*Smiles*) Men.

HANNAH

That's the trouble. It's a man's story. And men—excuse the expression—don't know shit. (*Beat*) Anyway, it's only a movie, right? Don't worry. You'll be fine.

CELIA

Well, there's no turning back now, is there?

46. INT: DAY. SOUNDSTAGE. THE SET OF *PANDORA'S BOX*.

What follows is a contemporary version of the last part of Act I of Earth Spirit. *It is set in a loft space.* BLACK, *the painter Schwarz from Wedekind's play, has been turned into a photographer. He has been taking pictures of* LULU. *She is dressed in a Charlie Chaplin costume: baggy trousers, tuxedo jacket, bowler hat, small fake mustache. Photography devices: screens, umbrellas, reflectors, standing lamps.*

The entire set is visible. Film crew, equipment, adjustable walls, etc. The scene begins with an overhead shot of CATHERINE *sitting in a chair and studying the monitor.*

She is flanked by the SCRIPT SUPERVISOR *and the* DIRECTOR OF PHOTOGRAPHY. *As the camera sweeps past her, she leans to her left and whispers something to the* D.P. *The camera continues to move, taking in the* SOUNDMAN, *the sound cart, and the* FIRST ASSISTANT DIRECTOR; *then, the* CAMERA OPERATOR, *the prop camera, the* FOCUS PULLER, *the* SECOND ASSISTANT CAMERAMAN *(clapper), and two* STAGEHANDS.

*Close-up of the clapper. It reads: "*PANDORA'S BOX. *Scene 3, Take 1."*

One by one, at the appropriate moments, we hear offscreen voices pronounce the following instructions:

FIRST ASSISTANT DIRECTOR (*off*)

Roll speed.

75

SOUNDMAN *(off)*

Speed.

FIRST ASSISTANT DIRECTOR *(off)*

Roll camera.

FIRST ASSISTANT CAMERAMAN *(off)*

Marker.

SECOND ASSISTANT CAMERAMAN *(off)*

Scene 3. Take 1. Mark.

Once the clapper has been lowered, we hear:

CATHERINE

(Calmly) Action.

A close-up of LULU'S *face. She begins twitching her nose.*

BLACK *(off)*

Hold still.

LULU

(Referring to the mustache) It itches. *(She wiggles her nose again)*

BLACK *(off)*

(Irritated) Stop it!

LULU

(Beat) I'm bored.

BLACK

Look, it wasn't my idea to take these dumb pictures.

LULU

It wasn't mine either, was it? Thank Peter Shine and his magazine for this. *(Beat)* At least you're getting paid.

She begins twitching her nose again. Impish, playful—perversely sabotaging the pose.

Master shot. BLACK *walks out from behind his tripod and approaches* LULU. *He is intensely irritated.*

BLACK

Can't you be good—just once?

LULU

(*Shrugs*) I'm good. I'm always good.

BLACK

We'll be here all day if you don't settle down.

LULU

You don't want to take my picture. You want to get inside my pants. (*Smiles*) You want to stick your tongue down my throat.

BLACK

(*Tormented, wavering*) Don't talk like that.

LULU

Why not? It's the truth, isn't it? If I'm wrong, then why aren't there any assistants around? (*Looks left; playfully*) Nobody there. (*Looks right*) Nobody there. (*Laughs*) It's just you and me, honey-pie.

BLACK

(*Losing control*) You're impossible.

LULU grins at him, as if egging him on, daring him to make a move. BLACK, *finally breaking down, impulsively grabs hold of her and kisses her on the mouth. She neither resists nor shows any enthusiasm.*

LULU

(*Teasing*) Oh, you bad man. (*Smiles, pulls off the face mustache*) Can't you wait until I turn back into a girl again? (*Tosses the mustache aside*)

They kiss again. LULU is more passionate this time. After a moment, however, she begins giggling. She disengages from BLACK and begins smacking her lips, as if trying to identify a taste.

LULU

Hmm. Garlic. (*Smacks her lips together again*) Or maybe . . . sausage. Hot sausage!

BLACK, deeply upset by now, looks at her with a mixture of horror and lust.

BLACK

Who the hell are you, anyway?

LULU

I'm me. That's who I am.

She takes off the bowler hat and tosses it aside. She runs her hand through her hair, shakes her head.

BLACK

What do you want?

LULU

(*Unbuttoning the jacket, taking it off, and tossing it aside*) I don't know.

BLACK

What do you believe in?

LULU

(*Sliding off her suspenders, undoing the button of her trousers*) I don't know. (*Beat*) Don't ask so many questions. I don't like it.

BLACK

Do you have a soul?

LULU

(*Lets the trousers drop, kicks them aside*) I don't know.

BLACK

Have you ever been in love?

LULU

(*Unbuttoning her shirt*) I don't know.

BLACK

(*Appalled*) You don't know?

LULU

(*Emphatic*) I don't know.

The camera moves in for a close-up of LULU's face. She continues unbuttoning the shirt. In the background we hear:

CATHERINE

And . . . cut.

CELIA's face relaxes as she comes out of character and returns to herself.

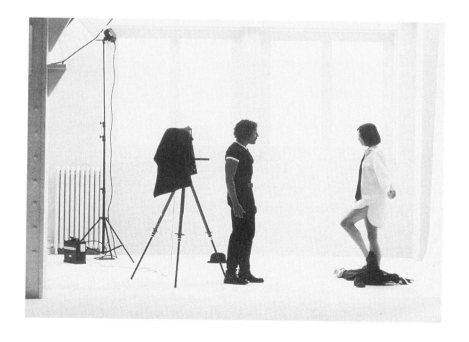

47. INT: NIGHT. THE ROOM.

IZZY, wide awake, is sitting on the floor with his back against a wall, hugging his knees. Dimness. To the degree that it is possible to make them out, his facial wounds appear to be much better.

After a few moments, sounds can be heard coming from outside the door. At first, an exchange of unintelligible voices, speaking in various foreign languages. The voices grow louder. Shouts are heard; an increasingly argumentative, violent tone. Then, followed by the sound of blows, bodies being thrown against the door.

Grunts, yelps, ever-mounting commotion. IZZY, afraid, confused, watches the door.

A line of bullets sweeps across the door, denting the metal surface. After that, all goes silent again.

IZZY crouches in the far corner of the room, terrified. We hear him breathing. A few moments go by. Then, with a great clattering of locks and bolts, the door abruptly swings open. A man enters: mid-forties, dressed in an elegant suit. This is DR. VAN HORN. As soon as he steps across the threshold, the door slams shut behind him. More clatter of locks and bolts. He is carrying a brown paper bag. He puts it down next to the door.

DR. VAN HORN

(*Calmly*) Hello, Mr. Maurer. I'm Dr. Van Horn.

IZZY

(*Slowly getting to his feet*) I can go now, right? (DR. VAN HORN *says nothing*) I mean, you're the good guys, aren't you? Isn't that what just happened? The good guys got rid of the bad guys?

DR. VAN HORN

Yes, we're the good guys.

IZZY

(*Beat. Not sure of what is going on*) I want to go home.

DR. VAN HORN

You will, I promise you. But we have to talk first. It's very important.

IZZY

(*Studying* DR. VAN HORN) I don't believe you.

DR. VAN HORN

(*Ignoring* IZZY's *remark. Begins sniffing the air*) It doesn't smell very good
in here, does it?

IZZY

A man has to shit. If he doesn't have a toilet, what do you expect?

DR. *VAN HORN casts his eyes about the room. Finally settles his gaze on one
shadowy corner—undoubtedly the spot where* IZZY *relieved himself.*

DR. VAN HORN

(*Thoughtful*) Montaigne once wrote: "Let us not forget that philoso-
phers and kings—and even ladies, too—must defecate."

IZZY

(*Harking back to his wish to go home*) Well?

DR. VAN HORN

(*Referring to the excrement*) Don't worry. I'll have it cleaned up. (*Beat.
Walks around a little*) You must be hungry. When was the last time
you ate?

IZZY

I don't want food. I just want to get out of here.

DR. VAN HORN

(*Sighs*) We're the good guys, Mr. Maurer, I can assure you of that.
What I want to know is whether you're good, too. (*Beat*) Are you
good, Mr. Maurer? Are you worthy?

IZZY

Worthy of what?

DR. VAN HORN

(*Pursuing his own line of thought*) I thought you could help us, you see. I had such high hopes for you. But I was wrong to trust you, wasn't I? (*Beat*) Am I right or wrong, Mr. Maurer?

IZZY

I don't know what you're talking about.

DR. VAN HORN

(*Firmly*) Yes you do. (*Beat. Looking* IZZY *in the eyes*) Stanley Mar, for one thing. And a little box he was carrying with him. Do you know how precious that stone is? (*Beat. Trying to control his emotions*) It took years to achieve that light. Do you have any idea of the good it can do? (*Falls silent, meditative. After a moment, he looks up again*) I'm so disappointed in you. (*Goes over to the paper bag and picks it up. Hands it roughly to* IZZY) Here. Change your clothes. You stink.

48. INT: DAY. SOUNDSTAGE. THE SET OF PANDORA'S BOX.

Unlike the previous extract from Pandora's Box *(scene 45), we do not experience the action as a movie within a movie but as the movie itself.*

A reworking of Act III of Earth Spirit, *combined with references to the theater scene in Pabst's film.*

(Background: LULU is performing in a rock 'n' roll concert. The other characters who appear in this section of the story are PETER SHINE [based on Dr. Schoen from the play], his fiancée MOLLY, and his son ALVIN [based on Alwa]. SHINE, in his late fifties or early sixties, is the publisher of a successful rock 'n' roll magazine. He has been involved with LULU for several years—at once irresistibly attracted to her and repulsed by her. For LULU, SHINE is the only man who counts, in spite of her numerous other conquests and liaisons. Finally, in an effort to break away from LULU once and for all and end their secret, on-again, off-again affair, SHINE has gotten himself engaged to MOLLY, an attractive but unremarkable young woman in her late twenties. Simultaneously, he has begun promoting LULU's career as a pop singer. ALVIN, his twenty-five-year-old son, has written and arranged her material.)

The scene takes place in LULU's dressing room—in a break between sets.

The dressing room is empty. The door opens. We hear loud cheering, clapping—a large audience giving an enthusiastic reception to the first part of LULU's concert. ALVIN rushes in, excited. A moment later, LULU enters as well. She looks flushed, happy, pleased with herself, nearly out of breath. She flops down in a chair.

ALVIN

Unbelievable. (*Uncorks a bottle of champagne*)

LULU

(*Catching her breath. Smiles*) They liked it, didn't they?

ALVIN

(*Pouring her a glass of champagne*) They went crazy. Where did you learn those moves?

LULU

(*Shrugs, as if to say she has no idea. Takes a sip of the champagne*) Is the other dress ready?

ALVIN

Relax. You have thirty minutes.

In the background, we hear music from another rock band coming from the stage. This music continues throughout the rest of the scene, punctuated by applause and cheering. An intense, chaotic atmosphere infuses the action.

LULU

(*Thinking*) This is just what Peter wanted, isn't it?

ALVIN

What do you mean?

LULU

He turns me into a success, and then, the more I succeed, the farther he can push me away from him. (*Beat*) It's his way of getting rid of me.

ALVIN

(*Sipping his champagne*) You don't know what you're talking about.

LULU

(*Slight pause*) Give me a cigarette.

ALVIN dutifully shakes out a cigarette from a pack on the table, lights it, and then hands it to LULU. She takes a drag.

ALVIN

He came tonight, you know. He's in the audience.

LULU

(*Feigning indifference*) He did? That's nice.

ALVIN

Just because he's marrying Molly, that doesn't mean he doesn't care about you.

LULU

He *thinks* he wants to marry her, but I'm the one he wants.

ALVIN shrugs, growing tired of the conversation. He looks at his watch. Just then, a knock is heard at the door. ALVIN walks across the room and opens it. It is PETER SHINE: hip, well-dressed, at ease with his own power.

ALVIN

Hi, Dad.

ALVIN leaves the door open and PETER pokes in his head. LULU looks up and gives him a blank stare. She doesn't greet him.

PETER

(*Smiling, to* LULU) What can I say? It's a breakthrough performance, Lulu. They'll be talking about it for months.

LULU

(*Coolly*) Let's hope so. If I danced any harder, I'd probably go into orbit.

The door opens a little wider and LULU catches sight of MOLLY, a pretty brunette, standing in the doorway with PETER.

LULU

(*Suddenly agitated, distraught*) What's she doing here?

PETER

She came to wish you luck for the second half.

MOLLY

(*Taking a step or two into the room, waving shyly to* LULU) Hi.

LULU

(*Ignoring* MOLLY; *boiling over with rage. To* PETER) You mean you actually brought her here? You mean she's actually been sitting next to you, watching me perform?

PETER

Why not? What difference does it make who sees you?

MOLLY

(*Beginning to grow upset; plucking up her courage*) I thought you were great, Lulu. I loved it.

LULU

(*Still addressing* PETER *and ignoring* MOLLY. *Exploding into a tantrum*) Get her out of my sight! Do you hear me! Get her out of here!

PETER

(*Trying to calm her down*) Take it easy. . . . You're getting all worked up over nothing . . .

ALVIN

(*Upset; to* PETER) Good work, Dad. Couldn't this have waited until after the show?

LULU

(*Hysterical*) I want her out of here! Out of my dressing room! Out of the theater! If she stays, I'm not going on! I'll cancel the rest of the show!

PETER

(*Shooing* ALVIN *and* MOLLY *out the door*) It's all right. I'll take care of it. (*Shutting the door firmly once they leave. Turning to* LULU) Stop acting like a baby. You disgust me. You're so incredibly . . . vulgar. (*Takes out a cigarette and puts it in his mouth*)

LULU

No smoking. (*Points to a* NO SMOKING *sign posted in the room*) Can't you read? I thought you owned a magazine.

PETER

(*Throws down the cigarette in disgust*) You signed a contract. You can't just walk out.

LULU

(*Long pause. The tension goes out of her; she slumps in her chair and closes her eyes. Wearily*) I'm so tired.

PETER

You'll go back on, then?

LULU

(*Eyes still closed; waving him off. As if to herself*) Yes, yes . . . I'll go back on. Now leave. I don't want you here anymore.

PETER

(*Wounded by her indifference*) Just like that?

LULU

(*Opens her eyes; gives him a cold, hard look*) Yes. Just like that.

PETER *doesn't move.* LULU, *understanding that she has just won an important victory, persists in the game she is playing.*

LULU

(*With a shooing gesture*) Go . . . go . . . go back to your sweet little Molly. (*Smiles knowingly*) Is that girl in for a surprise or what?

PETER

What's that supposed to mean?

LULU

When she finds out who you really are.

87

PETER

Stop it! (*Increasingly upset*) I'm finished with you.

LULU

You are, huh? And what happens six months from now when you've used that little girl up and start wanting me again? What happens when you pick up the phone in the middle of the night and dial my number? Do I answer it . . . or just let it ring?

PETER

(*Losing control. Raising his hand*) I should smack you. Right across the face!

LULU

(*Walking right up to him; brazenly; thrusting out her jaw*) Go ahead. Hit me. Come on, punch me as hard as you can. If that's what it takes for you to touch me again, then knock the living daylights out of me.

PETER, *overcome, realizes that he is lost, damned forever. He takes hold of* LULU's *face with his two hands, draws her toward him, and begins covering her with kisses.*

LULU, *luxuriating in her triumph, closes her eyes and leans back her head. A small inward smile spreads across her mouth as* PETER *kisses her neck.*

A moment later, the door opens. LULU *hears the sound and opens her eyes. Shot of the door:* ALVIN *and* MOLLY *are standing there, aghast. Pounding rock 'n' roll pours in from the stage.*

Shot of PETER's *back as he goes on kissing* LULU. *He stops, turns around, and looks* MOLLY *straight in the eyes. She begins to cry. Whatever hopes he had of breaking away from* LULU *have now been permanently destroyed.*

Then, suddenly breaking the spell, the background music goes silent. A voice calls out:

CATHERINE (*off*)
Cut!

Wide shot of the set. We see the crew and the equipment as we did in scene 45. The actors begin to relax.

CATHERINE
(*To the* SCRIPT SUPERVISOR) Let's print that one. But I want to have another go at it. Just give me a few minutes.

CATHERINE *walks away from the crew and enters the set. Long shot. We see her walk up to* CELIA, *who is leaning against a table, speak to her for a moment, and then lead her out of the dressing room. Once they leave the frame, cut to:*

CATHERINE *and* CELIA, *standing on the other side of the set partition wall.*

CATHERINE
It's still a little too broad . . .

CELIA
I was trying to hold back, but it's such an emotional scene . . .

89

CATHERINE

I know. It's all so over the top. But it's about real things. Hidden things, maybe, but things that are there. (*A beat, letting her words sink in*) You don't have to work so hard, Celia. Let the camera do it for you.

CELIA

(*Thinking, working it out for herself*) It's like turning dreams inside out, isn't it?

CATHERINE

We all have them in us. It's just a matter of how you let them go.

CELIA

(*Gently opening her hand—as if releasing a butterfly*) Like that?

CATHERINE

Exactly. And the camera will be there to show it.

Cut to:

49. INT: DAY. SOUNDSTAGE. A HALLWAY.

We see CELIA walking quickly down the corridor to her dressing room.

50. INT: DAY. CELIA'S DRESSING ROOM.

Frantic, CELIA sits down at the table, picks up the phone, and punches the keys for an international call. We hear the phone ringing. Eventually, an answering machine message comes on.

> IZZY'S VOICE
>
> Leave a message, and I'll get back to you.

> CELIA
>
> (*After the beep*) Izzy, where are you? They sent someone to the airport this morning to pick you up, and you weren't on the plane. Izzy, darling, what happened to you?

51. INT: DAY. SOUNDSTAGE. SOMEWHERE BEHIND THE SET.

A few moments later. BILLY (ALVIN) is standing alone against a wall, smoking a cigarette. CELIA, still in her LULU costume, walks into frame.

> BILLY
>
> Hi, Celia.

> CELIA
>
> (*Distracted*) Hi.

> BILLY
>
> Are you okay? (*Offers her a cigarette from his pack*)

> CELIA
>
> (*Stops, still distraught*) I'm fine. (*Pulls out a cigarette from the pack and puts it in her mouth*)

BILLY

(*Lighting the cigarette for her*) There's been a lot of talk, you know.

CELIA

Oh? About what?

BILLY

About you. (*Beat*) The word is that you have man troubles.

CELIA

Who said that?

BILLY

I can't remember. But I just wanted to say that—

CELIA

(*Interrupting him*) Don't believe everything you hear—

BILLY

Yeah, maybe so, but I just wanted to say that if there's any . . . any truth to the story, I just wanted to say—

CELIA

(*Cutting him off*)—Say what?

BILLY

That you don't have to be alone if you don't want to.

CELIA

What's that supposed to mean?

BILLY

That I'm here for you. Any time, any place . . . I'm here.

CELIA

(*Trying to control her emotions*) Fuck off, Billy. Just do your job, okay?

52. INT: DAY. THE ROOM.

Daylight slants through the window. A table has been set up in the middle of the room. DR. VAN HORN sits in a chair on one side; IZZY is in a chair on the other side. A desk lamp with a single bulb burning harshly between them.

IZZY is wearing a fresh set of clothes. Blue jeans, T-shirt, etc. A suggestion of prison garb.

In the far corner, a chamber pot. As promised, improvements have been made, but IZZY is still not free.

DR. VAN HORN has several folders in front of him. Every now and then, he opens one of them and scans the papers within. He is also equipped with a notepad and a pen. For reasons never made clear, he occasionally jots something down while IZZY talks. At other times, he appears to be doodling.

Everything about this scene escapes understanding. An air of mystery, doubt, disequilibrium. The same holds true of scenes 54 and 57.

DR. VAN HORN's purpose is never defined. At times, he appears to be conducting a police interrogation. At other times, he sounds like a psychiatrist. At still other times, he resembles the Grand Inquisitor.

> DR. VAN HORN
>
> Momentous things have happened, and whether you like it or not, you're in the middle of them.

> IZZY
>
> I don't have it. I told you that before. I don't have it, and I don't know where it is.

> DR. VAN HORN
>
> (*Changing the subject*) How long have you been here, Izzy?

> IZZY
>
> (*Shrugs*) What difference does it make? (*Beat*) Too long.

DR. VAN HORN

Answer the question. Days? Weeks? Months?

IZZY

I don't know. Days, I suppose. I can't remember how many.

DR. VAN HORN

What if I told you seven? What would you say to that?

IZZY

Nothing. I wouldn't say a thing.

DR. VAN HORN

When did you start using the name Izzy?

IZZY

(*Lets out a sigh*) This is ridiculous.

DR. VAN HORN

Your real name is Isaac, isn't it?

IZZY

So?

DR. VAN HORN

How old were you? Six? Eight? Fourteen?

IZZY

I don't remember.

DR. VAN HORN

But you do remember the fireflies, don't you?

IZZY

The what?

DR. VAN HORN

Maybe you called them lightning bugs. It doesn't matter. You know
what I'm talking about, don't you?

IZZY

No.

DR. VAN HORN

Those little things that fly around at night. In the summer, when the
weather is hot. Tiny pinpricks of light . . . going on and off . . . dart-
ing through the air . . . now in one place, now in another. Very beautiful, no?

IZZY

What is this, *Welcome to the World of Insects?*

DR. VAN HORN

No, it's called *Going Back,* or *Delving into the Past.* (*One or two beats;
prolonging* IZZY*'s confusion*) Remember Echo Lake? How many sum-
mers did you and your family go there?

IZZY

(*Taken completely by surprise. A little frightened. Several beats*) How do you know about that?

DR. VAN HORN

I know about a lot of things. (*Beat*) Do you remember the fireflies now?

IZZY

Yes. (*Beat*) Vaguely. (*Beat; coming clean*) Yes, I remember them.

DR. VAN HORN

You and your big brother would go out in the backyard at night, wouldn't you? Carrying jars with little holes punched in the top. (*Beat*) What was his name again?

IZZY

(*Very quietly; as if filled with dread*) Franz.

DR. VAN HORN

Yes, Franz, that's it. An interesting name. Franz. Franz and Isaac. How many years apart were you?

IZZY

(*With difficulty, barely able to get the word out of his mouth*) Three.

DR. VAN HORN

(*As if to himself*) Right. Three. Three years apart. (*Addressing* IZZY *again*) And so you and your big brother Franz, who was three years older than you, would go out at night to catch fireflies in the backyard. Your father punched the holes in the tops of the jars, didn't he? With a hammer and an eighth-inch nail. Tap, tap, tap. He was a doctor, your father, wasn't he? Not a pretend doctor like me, with my Ph.D. in anthropology, but an honest-to-goodness medical doctor, the kind who actually cures the sick and helps people get well. Stocky fellow, wasn't he? With strong upper arms, and one of those barrel chests. Bald, too, if I'm not mistaken, and even out there at the lake in the summer, when he had his one, measly week of holiday a year, he walked around in his white shirt, didn't he? No tie, of course, and he'd roll up his sleeves when the weather was particularly hot, but still, that's how you see him in your mind, isn't it? Your father in his white shirt.

IZZY

(*Suffering. Almost inaudible*) Stop it. Don't do this to me.

DR. VAN HORN

(*Ignoring him*) So there you'd be, you and Franz, running around the backyard of the house by Echo Lake trying to catch fireflies and put them in your jars. It was so magnificent, holding that jar in your hand with all those flickering lights inside, and of course the more fireflies you caught and put in the jar, the more impressive and beautiful the lantern would be. The problem was that you weren't very good at catching fireflies. Every time you reached out for one, it would suddenly go dark, and then another would light up somewhere else, distracting you from the first one just long enough to lose track of where it was. So you would go after the second one, and the same thing would happen all over again. And again; and again. Meanwhile, your big brother Franz, who was three years older than you, would be snaring one incandescent bug after another. His jar would be glowing like a small temple of dreams. And again and again you would come up empty-handed. It drove you into spasms of frustration, and the more you continued to fail, the more desperate you became. Finally— in your sniveling, abject little way—you would resort to tears, raising such a fuss that your mother would have to come running outside, your poor mother who was spending a few tranquil moments with your father in the house, your father drinking his one nightly beer in his white shirt with the sleeves rolled up, and nine times out of ten she would settle things by forcing a reluctant, belligerent Franz to part with a few of his fireflies so you'd have something to put in your jar, too. Anything to keep the brat quiet. Right, Izzy? Anything for a few moments of peace.

IZZY

(*On the point of tears*) What kind of a man are you?

DR. VAN HORN

(*Ignoring* IZZY's *question*) When was the last time you saw Franz?

IZZY

I don't want to talk about this.

DR. VAN HORN

Answer the question. (*Beat*) You have to answer the question.

IZZY

(*Beginning to cry*) I don't know.

DR. VAN HORN

Seven years ago, that's when. He asked you to play at your father's funeral, and you refused. Why did you do a thing like that? Who the hell do you think you are? Your brother hates you so much, he didn't even bother to visit you in the hospital after you were shot. (*Beat*) You've burned a lot of bridges in your day, haven't you?

IZZY, *cracking under the verbal assault, buries his face in his hands and sobs.*

53. INT: DAY. SOUNDSTAGE. THE SET OF *PANDORA'S BOX.*

The scene takes place in SHINE *and* LULU's *bedroom. They have been married for a year. On one wall, we see a photograph of* LULU *in the Charlie Chaplin costume.*

CATHERINE *is blocking out the scene with* CELIA, TOM (*the actor who plays* PETER SHINE), *and* BILLY (ALVIN), *going through a last rehearsal before attempting the first take.* CELIA *is wearing a skimpy white dress.* TOM (SHINE) *is wearing elegant dress clothes—a tuxedo, or some suitable variation.* BILLY (ALVIN) *is dressed casually.*

CATHERINE

All right, that was good. Let's do it one more time, just to make sure you have the blocking down. Remember, Tom, the scene begins with the door swinging open—and then the shove. Celia gets thrown onto the bed, and you . . . (*she walks to a spot in the room and points to the floor*) . . . and you stop here, right where this tape is (*points down to the tape*). That will make it simpler for you to go to the bureau (*points to the bureau*) and take out the gun. (*Turning to* BILLY) Billy, I'll give you a signal when you're supposed to knock. Right after Tom says, "Now do what you have to do. Do it." Okay? Everything clear?

CELIA, TOM, *and* BILLY *nod. As they go to their places on the other side of the bedroom door, the* FIRST ASSISTANT DIRECTOR *whispers something in* CATHERINE's *ear. She nods. Then, once the actors are in their positions:*

CATHERINE

(*As soon as things seem quiet*) Action.

The scene unfolds primarily from CATHERINE's *POV, with occasional reaction shots of* CATHERINE *watching the actors. The scene feels more like theater than film, and the artificiality of the environment is felt throughout.*

The door flies open. PETER, *holding a resistant, angry* LULU *by the arm, flings her onto the bed.*

LULU

(*Protesting*) But I want to go!

PETER

We're not going anywhere!

LULU

But you promised!

PETER

For what? So you can go and pick up somebody else to sleep with?

LULU

(*Denying everything*) You're out of your mind. (*Getting off the bed*)

PETER

You think I don't know? You think I don't know about that doped-up drummer—and the hockey player—and that dyke painter you've been hanging around with? (*Exploding*) You think I don't know?

LULU

(*Calmly*) I married *you,* didn't I? If I wanted them, why would I marry you?

PETER

(*Ignoring her question; pursuing his own argument*) I could forget all that—pretend to ignore it—but when you start messing around with my own son—then that's—going—too—far!

LULU

I can't help what Alvin feels, Peter . . .

PETER, *continuing to ignore what she says, goes over to the bureau, opens the top drawer, and takes out a pistol.*

He came on to me, but I turned him down, and that's the god's honest truth. If you don't believe me, go ask him yourself.

PETER

(*Turning around and pointing the gun at her. On the brink of hysteria*) Do you see this?

LULU, not taking him seriously, does not answer. SHINE *repeats the question at the top of his voice.*

PETER

Do you see it!

LULU

Yes, I see it.

PETER

(*Forcing the gun into her hand*) Take it!

LULU

(*Resisting*) Stop it, Peter.

PETER

(*Redoubling his efforts*) Take it.

She finally relents, takes hold of the gun.

PETER

I want to cure myself. Do you understand? And this . . . this is the medicine.

LULU

(*Laughs nervously*) I'm not going to shoot you.

PETER

Not me, darling—you. There's no other way. If you don't do it, then there's no hope for me . . . no hope for Alvin . . . no hope for any of us.

LULU

(*Pointing the gun at him*) It's not loaded.

PETER

Oh no?

LULU points the gun at the ceiling and pulls the trigger. CELIA, providing the sound effect, says "Bang."

LULU

(*Growing scared*) Look Peter, if you've had enough, we can split up . . . get a divorce.

PETER

(*Laughs bitterly*) We're so far beyond divorce, I don't even know what that word means anymore. (*Beat. With madness in his eyes*) Till death do us part, Lulu. (*Furious at her refusal to go along with him. Tries to tear the gun out of her hands*) Here, give it to me. If you won't do it yourself, I'll do it for you.

LULU

(*Struggling to hold on to the gun*) No, Peter. Stop it.

PETER

(*Out of his mind*) Do you think I care? Do you think I give a damn anymore? (*Lunges at her*)

LULU backs away from him. When she is at a safe distance from him, she lowers the gun.

LULU

(*In a decisive, self-confident tone*) I can't help what other people do, Peter, but I've never been anyone but myself. You know that, and everyone else knows that. Don't turn me into something I'm not. I can't stand all these lies.

(*Rushes at* LULU, *grabs hold of her shoulders, and forces her to the ground*) On your knees . . . monster! (*Points the barrel of the gun, which is still in* LULU's *hand, at* LULU *herself*) Now do what you have to do! Do it!

Suddenly—a frantic knocking is heard at the door.

ALVIN (*off*)

Dad. Are you all right?

PETER, *distracted by his son's voice, wheels in the direction of the door. His back is turned to* LULU.

PETER

Alvin . . .

LULU *points the gun at* PETER's *back. Again,* CELIA *provides the sound effects. Close-up of her face as she pretends to fire off the five bullets left in the chamber.*

LULU / CELIA

Bang. Bang. Bang. Bang. Bang.

Cut to:

54. INT: DAY. SOUNDSTAGE. SET OF *PANDORA'S BOX.*

The day's shooting is over. CELIA, *out of costume, is sitting in the* SHINE/ LULU *bedroom with* PHILIP, HANNAH, *and* CATHERINE. *She is clearly in distress over* IZZY's *failure to appear. We catch them in midconversation.*

HANNAH

Izzy's unpredictable, yes, but he wouldn't do a thing like this.

CELIA

Something's happened to him. I know it. He's in trouble.

PHILIP

Or else he changed his mind. I mean, you never know, do you?

HANNAH

Shut up, Philip.

PHILIP

(*To* HANNAH) I'm just trying to look at all the possibilities. (*To* CELIA) If you want, I'll call New York in the morning and get someone to start looking for him.

CATHERINE, who has been listening to the others with growing concern, finally enters the conversation.

CATHERINE

(*To* CELIA) Tomorrow's Sunday. What are you going to do with yourself?

CELIA

I don't know. I haven't been able to think that far ahead.

CATHERINE

Don't sit around and sulk. Will you promise me that? We have some
demanding scenes on Monday and Tuesday, and you need to have a
clear head.

CELIA

I'll be all right.

CATHERINE

(*Studying* CELIA) Love affairs come and go, but the work is what lasts.
You know that, don't you?

CELIA

(*Defiantly*) No, I don't think I do. I don't think I know anything.

55. INT: DAY. THE ROOM.

The room, as before. Dusk slants through the window.

*IZZY and DR. VAN HORN sitting at opposite sides of the table, as before. In the
background, we see that certain improvements have been made. There is a cot,
for example, and a washstand with a basin of water on it, and a peg on the
wall with an extra pair of pants hanging from it.*

The scene begins in midconversation. DR. VAN HORN *is looking through one
of the folders in front of him.*

DR. VAN HORN

. . . and on June fourteenth of the following year, ten dollars were
missing from your mother's purse. May twenty-ninth, the year after
that, you cheated your way through an algebra exam by copying the
answers from a girl who sat next to you. Susan Morse—that was her
name, wasn't it? She had a crush on you, and so you led her along to
make sure you wouldn't flunk the course and have to go to summer
school. Nice work, my friend. Susan must have felt quite happy when
you stopped talking to her the day after the test.

IZZY

(*Almost inaudible*) I hated school. I was a terrible student.

DR. VAN HORN

(*With a wave of the hand. Closing the folder; opening another*) These are paltry things . . . hardly worth mentioning . . . but they show a certain pattern, don't they? (*Flipping through the contents of the second folder*) Out of little seeds do mighty trees grow. (*Studying an entry on one of the pages*) Ah. (*Taps his fingers on the page*) This little piece of nastiness interests me. December fourth, six years ago. The Paradise Lounge, Milwaukee, Wisconsin. You and your band performed there that night, didn't you? Do you remember a man named Jack Bartholemew?

IZZY

(*Defensive*) We settled out of court.

DR. VAN HORN

I know that. But you didn't have to break his arm, did you?

IZZY

The guy stiffed us. He begs us to play his lousy club in Milwaukee in the middle of the goddamn winter, and the night we go on there's a snowstorm and nobody shows up. So the son-of-a-bitch decides not to pay us. We didn't even have enough money to get back to New York. (*Beat*) So I lost my temper.

DR. VAN HORN

You loved playing with that band, didn't you?

IZZY

It was my whole life.

DR. VAN HORN

You shouldn't have given up music, Izzy.

IZZY

I didn't. It gave me up. (*Beat*) I got shot, remember? (*Another beat. Gets up from his chair and walks toward the cot*) I'm tired of this. (*Sitting down on the cot*) I don't want to be here anymore.

DR. VAN HORN

(*Unfazed. Changing the subject*) What else to you care about, Izzy? Besides yourself, that is.

IZZY

Care? What do you mean care?

DR. VAN HORN

I don't know. Anything. Art. Literature. Collecting stamps. French wines. Astrology.

IZZY

I'm not interested in these questions.

DR. VAN HORN

Come on, Izzy. Indulge me.

IZZY

(*Shrugs. Thinks for a moment. Then, slyly*) Women. Women's bodies. Having sex with women.

DR. VAN HORN

(*Smiling*) Good. (*Beat*) What else?

IZZY

Nothing. Besides music, that's it.

DR. VAN HORN

(*Thoughtful*) What's your favorite book?

IZZY

I don't have a favorite book.

107

DR. VAN HORN

What's your favorite movie?

IZZY

I don't like movies. I never go to them.

DR. VAN HORN

I thought every American loved the movies.

IZZY

Not me. I used to go . . . when I was a kid. But then Gene Kelly retired, and the joy kind of went out of it for me. He's dead now, you know.

DR. VAN HORN

(*For the first time a little surprised*) You're not pulling my leg, are you? You really like Gene Kelly?

IZZY

(*Thinking about it*) Yeah. As a matter of fact, I do.

DR. VAN HORN

Which film? Which song?

IZZY

I don't know. Most of them, I guess. But my favorite number would have to be *Singin' in the Rain.* I never get tired of it. Every time I see it, it's just as great as the time before.

DR. VAN HORN

(*Smiling, sympathetic*) For once I agree with you. I love it, too. In fact, I would even go so far as to say it's one of the finest, most beautiful things ever created by an American. As good as the Declaration of Independence. As good as *Moby Dick.*

IZZY

Shit, it's better than that stuff. *Singin' in the Rain* is forever.

DR. VAN HORN gets out of his chair and walks toward IZZY's cot, smiling. Stops in the middle of the room. Then, in a dignified, almost nostalgic manner, he begins to do a soft shoe dance and to sing in a quiet voice.

DR. VAN HORN

I'm singin' in the rain / I'm singin' in the rain / What a glorious feelin' / I'm happy again . . .

The scene ends with a close shot of his face.

56. INT: NIGHT. DUBLIN. CELIA'S HOTEL ROOM.

Sunday. Early evening. CELIA has spent her day off alone, hiding out in her apartment.

The scene begins with CELIA entering the living room with the small black box in her hands.

She walks around the room, pulling down shades and closing curtains, then switches off the overhead light. One lamp is still on next to the sofa. She sits down on the sofa, puts the black box on the coffee table in front of her, takes the stone out of the box, puts the stone on the table, and switches off the lamp. Obscurity.

After a few moments, the stone begins to glow with the same blue light as before. Little by little, the light intensifies, grows more beautiful. CELIA watches. After a few more moments, the stone rises a few inches off the table. Then, a few moments after that, the stone divides in two.

Two glowing blue objects hover above the table.

In the radiant blue light that has flooded the room, we see tears rolling down CELIA's cheeks.

CELIA

(*Barely above a whisper*) What happened, Izzy? Where are you?

She begins crying in earnest, overwhelmed by sorrow. After a few moments, no longer able to bear it, she reaches out abruptly and turns on the lamp. The room fills with light. The humble, ordinary stone is sitting on the table. Sobbing now, CELIA gently puts the stone in the box and covers it. It is as if, in this solemn gesture, she has just buried IZZY. She looks at the box for a moment. Then, still sobbing, she stands up, opens all the curtains and blinds, and turns on the overhead light.

A few moments later, unable to contain her misery, she puts on her coat, picks up the black box from the coffee table, and leaves the apartment. The door closes behind her.

57. EXT: NIGHT. DUBLIN STREETS.

Various shots of CELIA walking through the city. The streets are utterly deserted. The sound of her footsteps ringing against the pavement.

After a time, CELIA walks through Merchants' Arch and comes to the Ha'penny Bridge, a pedestrian bridge that spans the Liffey. She goes up the steps and begins to walk across. At the exact center of the bridge, she stops.

Wide shot, from a distance. Close shot of CELIA's *face. Shot of the river below from* CELIA's POV.

CELIA takes the stone out of the box, then looks around to make sure that no one is watching. Holding the stone in her right hand, her arm fully extended, she leans over the edge.

Two, three beats. She opens her hand and lets the stone fall into the water.

58. INT: NIGHT. THE ROOM.

The room, as before. IZZY *is sitting on his cot, reading a paperback copy of Tolstoy's* Resurrection. *A small lamp burns beside him. On the floor, a tray with dishes on it: the remains of* IZZY's *dinner.*

The sound of locks and bolts being turned. IZZY *looks up.* DR. VAN HORN *enters.*

DR. VAN HORN
(*Taking his seat at the table. Sternly*) Come here, Izzy.

IZZY

(*Reluctant*) Don't you ever sleep?

DR. VAN HORN

We don't have much time. (*Pointing to the chair opposite him*) Sit.

IZZY dog-ears a page in the Tolstoy novel, closes the book, and puts it down on the pillow. He stands up and walks to his seat.

IZZY

(*Taking his seat. Warily*) Is something wrong?

DR. VAN HORN

Everything is wrong. (*Beat*) Because of you.

IZZY

(*Sarcastically*) And I thought you were beginning to like me. (*Beat*) Silly me.

DR. VAN HORN

I was. But feelings have nothing to do with this. I can't trust you.

IZZY

Why not? I've been telling you the truth. Every word I've said . . . is true.

Reverse angle shot from over DR. VAN HORN's shoulder. We see him writing the letters of CELIA's name: C-E-L-I-A.

DR. VAN HORN

So you say. But the words of a liar don't mean anything. They have no credibility.

IZZY

Look, I'm not stupid. You know too much about me for me to lie to you.

DR. VAN HORN

(*Shaking his head*) You're not worthy. You've led a bad, dishonest life.

IZZY

I'm not going to argue with you. (*Beat. In a more somber register*) But then I got shot. You'd think that would be the worst thing that could have happened to me, but it wasn't. I've changed since then. I've let go . . . of my rottenness. I've been trying to be different.

DR. VAN HORN

(*Sarcastically*) A new man.

IZZY

(*Sincerely*) Maybe. I don't know what to call it. But I feel more connected to things now. More connected to other people. Responsible, somehow.

DR. VAN HORN

(*With deep bitterness*) Then why haven't you helped me? (*Long beat, staring at* IZZY) Why haven't you told me about Celia Burns?

IZZY

(*Completely thrown*) Who?

DR. VAN HORN

You heard me.

IZZY

I don't know that person. (*Beginning to recover his wits. Understanding that he must protect* CELIA *at all costs*) What did you say her name was?

DR. VAN HORN

(*With quiet determination*) I could have you killed, you know. All I have to do is bang on the door, and a man will come in here with a gun and put a bullet through your head.

IZZY

(*Sighs*) Been there, done that.

DR. VAN HORN

Sounds like the old Izzy to me.

IZZY

Well, habits die hard.

Reverse angle shot from over DR. VAN HORN's *shoulder as he speaks. We see him writing on his pad: Celia—Celia—Ce-li-a—S'il y a.*

DR. VAN HORN

If you'd told me right away, the whole situation could have been saved. Now it's probably too late. (*Beat. Making one last appeal*) What if I told you that this is your one chance to do some good in the world? (*Beat. No response from* IZZY. *Tries a new approach*) Tell me about her, Izzy, and I'll let you go. I'll unlock the door, and you'll be free.

IZZY

I wish I could . . . but I don't know this person you're talking about.

DR. VAN HORN

(*Exploding with rage. Slamming his palm down on the table*) Of course you do! You're in love with her!

IZZY

(*Still playing dumb*) I am?

DR. VAN HORN

(*Abruptly standing up. Beside himself*) That's it. I have nothing more to say to you. (*Begins walking to the door. Stops*) You won't be seeing me again. (*Beat*) And without me, you're lost. (*Continues walking. Bangs on door. Turns to* IZZY *one last time*) May God have mercy on your soul.

The door opens. DR. VAN HORN *walks out. The door shuts. The clatter of locks and bolts being turned.*

59. INT: NIGHT. LULU'S APARTMENT. THE SET OF *PANDORA'S BOX.*

CATHERINE, *the crew, and the equipment are not visible. We experience what happens as unmediated action.*

A variation on Act III of Wedekind's Pandora's Box. *The scene has been shifted from London to the Lower East Side of Manhattan. Following the killing of Peter Shine, Lulu and Alvin have run away. They are destitute, living in the most squalid conditions. Alvin has become addicted to cocaine; Lulu occasionally resorts to prostitution in order to feed them—and to feed Alvin's habit. Alvin does not approve, but he is too weak to stop her.*

Night. It is raining outside. We are in the living room of a tawdry slum apartment. Plaster cracks in the wall; peeling paint; a few pieces of battered, secondhand furniture. There are several leaks in the ceiling. Basins and kitchen pots have been placed on the floor to catch the water, but they are all full, about to overflow. The only light comes from a single bare bulb hanging on a string from the ceiling.

115

ALVIN, looking disheveled, with long stringy hair, a motorcycle jacket, and his shirt tails hanging out of his pants, is sitting at a table, trying to gather his few last bits of cocaine into a pile big enough to snort. He appears to be on the edge of desperation.

The front door opens, and LULU enters the room. She looks wet, ragged. She is dressed all in black: miniskirt, tights, boots, and a motorcycle jacket similar to ALVIN's. She shuts the door with her foot, shaking out a cheap, partly torn umbrella as she walks in. She tries to close the umbrella, can't get the catch to work, and tosses it on the floor. ALVIN studies her intently but doesn't say a word.

She walks over to the table, reaches into her jacket pocket, pulls out a wad of bills, and tosses it onto the table in front of ALVIN.

ALVIN

Where'd you get it?

LULU

You don't want to know. (*Walks away from the table and starts removing her jacket. When it is half off, she puts it back on*) Christ, it's cold in here.

ALVIN

Up to your old tricks again, huh?

LULU

What do you care? You don't have to watch.

She walks in the direction of a bright red plastic armchair, sees a bottle of bourbon sitting on the floor, and picks it up. Drinks straight from the bottle. After a couple of swigs, a knock is heard at the door.

LULU

Who's that?

ALVIN

How should I know? (*Beat. As an afterthought*) One of your admirers, maybe.

116

LULU goes to answer the door. She opens it on CANDY *(based on Countess Geschwitz from the play), a Lower East Side lesbian painter with a crush on* LULU. *She is dressed in black leather; several facial piercings.*

LULU

(*To* CANDY; *without much enthusiasm*) Oh, it's you.

ALVIN

See? What did I tell you?

CANDY

(*To* LULU) Hi, sweetheart. Can I come in for a minute? I have a present for you.

LULU lets her in without saying anything. CANDY *is carrying a poster tube under her arm. As she takes off her coat, she eyes* ALVIN *with a sarcastic smile.*

CANDY

Well, if it isn't Alvin Shine, Captain Inertia himself.

ALVIN

(*Unfazed. With humor*) Hey there, Butch. Take a load off.

CANDY

(*Sliding a poster out of the tube*) I went into one of those poster stores today, and look what I found.

She unrolls the poster and holds it up. It is a picture from the Charlie Chaplin photo shoot with BLACK *in scene 45. In this shot,* LULU *is without the mustache. The bowler hat is pushed to the back of her head, the jacket is open, the shirt is partly open, and* LULU *is smiling a broad, fetching smile.*

LULU

(*Under her breath*) Oh, Jesus. Get that out of here.

ALVIN

(*Getting up from his seat*) Ah, the good old days. (*Walks toward* CANDY)

CANDY

(*Still holding up the poster*) I think it's beautiful.

117

ALVIN

(*Looking from the poster to* LULU *and back to the poster*) And just look, she hasn't changed a bit! (*Grabs hold of* LULU's *chin—a little too brusquely—and turns it toward the poster*)

LULU

Stop it.

ALVIN

(*Still holding her chin*) Think of all she's lived through, and the childlike expression in her eyes is still the same.

CANDY

Leave her alone, Alvin.

ALVIN

(*Getting excited*) We have to hang it up! (*Snatches the poster from* CANDY) That's what we need around here—some decoration! A picture like this . . . will inspire us! The goddess . . . of the temple of flesh! (*Laughs*)

He rushes over to a wall, sees a nail sticking out of it, and tries to pin the poster to the nail. The poster falls to the ground.

118

ALVIN

Shit.

CANDY

Take the nail out of the wall, stupid.

Just then, the light goes out. The room is plunged into darkness.

We can dimly make out the shapes of the three figures.

ALVIN

Great. Now I can't even see.

LULU

I'll go get a candle. (*Disappears into the bedroom*)

CANDY

(*To* ALVIN) You're such a clown, Alvin.

LULU comes back carrying a short, lighted candle on a saucer. The camera moves toward her as she moves toward the camera. A close-up of the light flickering against her face, her eyes. Cut to:

60. EXT: NIGHT. THE STREET BELOW. THE SET OF *PANDORA'S BOX*.

Standing across from LULU's building is JACK. Mid-thirties; leather jacket; dead eyes. He stands there looking up at the building across the street. An addict stumbles by . . . a pair of punk kids.

Shot of the third floor window. A candle is burning on the sill.

Shot of JACK, waiting. He opens his jacket, checks the inside pocket, pats it with his hand.

Shot of the building across the street. We see ALVIN come out, look around, and walk left out of frame.

Shot of JACK. He follows ALVIN with his eyes for a moment, then folds his arms across his chest and leans his back against the wall. Cut to:

61. INT: NIGHT. LULU'S APARTMENT. THE SET OF *PANDORA'S BOX*.

LULU and CANDY are sitting in chairs, talking, waiting for ALVIN to return with a lightbulb. In the meantime, the candle provides the only light.

CANDY

I don't know why you stay with him.

LULU

I made a promise, that's why. (*Beat*) You wouldn't understand.

CANDY

I understand. I also understand that the night we spent together was the happiest night of my life.

LULU

What happened that night doesn't mean anything. I was curious, that's all. But now it's over.

CANDY *begins to cry at the bluntness of* LULU's *statement.*

LULU

Just pretend it never happened. (*Beat. As* CANDY *continues to cry*) I'm just telling the truth. It's better that way.

CANDY

(*After a moment. Sniffing back her tears*) That's why I love you, Lulu. There's never any bullshit with you, is there?

A knock is heard at the door.

LULU

Alvin. He probably forgot his key. (*Gets up and walks to the door*)

CANDY

(*Trying to put up a brave front. Still tearful*) How many morons does it take to screw in a light bulb?

LULU

(*Laughs. Over her shoulder*) He probably forgot the light bulb, too.

LULU *opens the door.* JACK *is standing in the hall.*

LULU

(*Recovering from her surprise. Smiling*) Hello. And who are you?

JACK

I saw you down on the street before. I followed you here.

LULU

Do you have a name?

JACK

Jack. (*Beat*) You can call me Jack. (*Steps into the apartment.* LULU *closes the door. Then, seeing* CANDY) Who's that?

LULU

My sister. She's a little crazy. I can't get her to leave.

JACK

(*Looking at* LULU) You have a beautiful mouth.

LULU

(*Smiling*) A gift from my mother.

JACK

How much? I don't have a lot of money.

LULU

I don't know. . . . Fifty dollars.

JACK

(*Turning to the door. As if about to leave*) So long. I'll be seeing you.

LULU

No, don't go. (*Putting her hand on his arm. He looks down at her hand with a curiously remote expression on his face*) Please stay.

JACK

How much?

LULU

Half, then. Twenty-five dollars.

JACK

That's still too much.

CANDY

(*Watching and listening to them with growing astonishment and disgust*) Christ, I don't believe this. Pretty soon, you'll be paying *him*.

LULU

(*To* CANDY) Shut up.

JACK

(*Walking over to* CANDY. *Studies her. They exchange a long look. Then, to* LULU) That's not your sister. She's in love with you. (*Pats* CANDY*'s head*) Nice doggy. (*Then, walking back toward* LULU, *studying her intently*)

LULU

Why are you looking at me like that?

JACK

The first thing that caught my eye was your walk. I said to myself, "That girl has a great body."

LULU

How can you know that?

JACK

And I saw that you had a pretty mouth. (*Beat*) I have only ten dollars.

LULU

All right, what's the difference?

JACK

I'll need some of it back, though. For subway fare.

CANDY

(*Getting up from her seat and walking to the far end of the room*) I can't stand this, Lulu. I really can't stand this. (JACK *and* LULU *ignore her*)

LULU

I don't have change for a ten. I don't have anything.

JACK

Look in your pockets. You must have something.

LULU

(*Plunges a hand into each pocket of her jacket and fishes around inside. Pulls out a crumpled five-dollar bill*) This is all I have.

123

JACK

Give it to me.

LULU

I'll get change later. After we're done.

JACK

No, I want it all.

LULU

All right, all right. For God's sake—take it. (*She gives it to him*) But let's go into the bedroom now. (*Walks over to the candle and picks it up*)

JACK

We don't need that. It's bright enough.

LULU

(*Putting down the candle*) All right. Whatever you say. (*Walks over to* JACK *and puts her arms around him*) I won't hurt you. I really like you. Don't make me beg anymore.

JACK

Okay. Let's go.

JACK *follows* LULU *into the bedroom.* CANDY *lights a cigarette and walks around the living room—agitated, disturbed. After a few moments, terrible piercing screams are heard from the bedroom.*

LULU (*off*)

Help! . . . Help!

CANDY *rushes to the bedroom door.*

CANDY

(*Desperately*) Lulu! Lulu!

124

JACK rushes out of the bedroom with a long, bloodstained knife in his right hand. He plunges it into CANDY's belly. She lets out a grunt of surprise and pain and then totters backward. JACK catches her with his left hand and holds her up. With his right hand, he sticks the knife into her again—and then again.

Traveling shot. The camera moves in on JACK and then, slowly, sweeps past him into the bedroom. LULU is sitting on the floor, her back against the bed, clutching her stomach.

LULU

Oh Jesus . . . Oh Jesus.

The life is quickly draining out of her. The camera moves in on her face. A far-off look. A look deep within. The look of a person about to die.

62. INT: DAY. THE ROOM.

The room, as before. It is morning.

IZZY is pounding on the metal door with his right hand. No one comes.

(*Shouting*) Help! Please—someone—help me!

Nothing happens. After a while, he stops pounding on the door and sinks to his knees. Two or three seconds; breathing hard. Then, mustering his strength, he stands up and staggers over to the table. He grabs hold of the table and pushes it against the wall under the window. He climbs onto the table, stands up, and reaches for the window. He can touch it with his hand, but he isn't high enough to see it. He climbs down from the table, picks up one of the chairs, and puts it on the table. Then he climbs back onto the table himself, pushes the back of the chair against the wall, and climbs onto the chair. This time, he is high enough. He pounds the window with his fist. The glass is thick, unbreakable. He climbs down again, carefully lowering himself from the chair to the table to the floor, and gathers up the silverware from his food tray. He climbs back onto the table, then onto the chair, holding a knife, fork, and spoon in his hand. He takes the knife and begins stabbing at the edges of the window. Cut to:

63. EXT: DAY. DUBLIN. OUTSIDE CELIA'S HOTEL.

It is early morning. We see CELIA *leave the building dressed in casual clothes, a bag slung over her shoulder. She turns left and begins walking. After a few moments, as if appearing out of nowhere,* DR. VAN HORN *suddenly enters the frame from the opposite direction.*

> DR. VAN HORN

Celia Burns?

> CELIA

(Startled. Stops walking) Yes?

> DR. VAN HORN

May I have a word with you, please?

> CELIA

(Starts walking again) I'm sorry. I have to be at the set in fifteen minutes.

DR. VAN HORN *walks quickly beside her, trying to keep up with her. Until now, we have seen them from the side.*

The angle changes at this moment and we see them from the front, walking briskly down the pavement. Behind, at a distance of about ten feet, TWO LARGE MEN *in windbreakers are following them.*

> DR. VAN HORN

It's about Izzy Maurer. He wants to see you.

> CELIA

(Stopping dead in her tracks. The TWO MEN *following also stop. Astonished, delighted)* Izzy? You know where he is?

> DR. VAN HORN

I do. If you come with me now, I can take you right to him.

CELIA

(*Laughing; full of hope; confused*) They're expecting me. Let me call first. I don't want them to worry.

DR. VAN HORN

(*Taking her by the elbow and turning her around*) There's a phone in the car.

CELIA

(*Seeing the* TWO LARGE MEN *for the first time*) Who are they?

DR. VAN HORN

Don't worry. They're with me.

CELIA *suddenly grows suspicious, afraid. A series of very quick close-ups of* CELIA's *face,* DR. VAN HORN's *face, and the faces of the* TWO MEN. *At one point, trying to put her at ease, the* TWO MEN *smile at her. One of them is missing his front teeth; the other one is wearing metal braces. The effect is gruesome.* CELIA *begins to back away from them.*

CELIA

I get it. (*Backing away some more*) I know what you want now. (*Removing her purse from her shoulder as she continues to back away*) It's in here.

She throws the bag at one of the MEN, *and takes off running as fast as she can.*

DR. VAN HORN *and the* TWO MEN *rummage through the bag for a few moments, flinging objects onto the ground: a makeup bag, a magazine, a paperback book (* Lulu in Hollywood *by Louise Brooks), tissues, hairbrush, the Katmandu CD. This gives* CELIA *a small head start on them.*

Long shot: CELIA *runs down the street and out of frame. As* DR. VAN HORN *sifts through the contents of the bag, the* TWO MEN *chase after her.*

64. EXT: DAY. THE CITY STREETS.

Following the same route that CELIA *took in scene 56 on her way to the bridge, the chase continues through the streets of the city. Alternating long shots and close shots. It is six o'clock in the morning. The streets are not very crowded—but nevertheless, some traffic, some pedestrians, a number of physical obstacles.*

Finally, CELIA *reaches the Ha'penny Bridge. She runs up the steps. She is only twenty or thirty feet in front of the* MEN. *She begins running down the walkway; the* MEN *run up the steps. Halfway across, at the same spot from which she dropped the stone into the water,* CELIA *stops running. Exhausted, out of breath. The* TWO MEN *are gaining on her by the second.*

Not knowing what else to do or how else to escape them, she climbs up onto the railing just as they are about to catch her. A long moment. She hesitates. A shot of the water below. A shot of CELIA's *face. A shot of one of the* MEN. *He reaches out his hand, as if to help her down.*

MAN

Don't do it, miss. We're not going to hurt you.

Nevertheless, CELIA *jumps.*

The scene ends with a long shot of CELIA *flying through the air and landing in the water. We see the splash—and then she goes under.*

65. INT: DAY. THE ROOM.

The room, as before. IZZY, *still standing on the chair, is hammering away at the handle of the knife with one of the legs from the other chair. Most of the glass in the window is now missing. Just one jagged piece remains. Grunting with each blow he strikes,* IZZY *finally knocks a large chunk free. Then, very carefully, he uses his fingers to slide the last shard from the window frame. Without hesitating or looking back, he hoists himself up and begins to climb through the hole.*

66. EXT: DAY. WAREHOUSE BUILDING/BROOKLYN.

From the outside of the building, we see IZZY *climb through the window. It is just above ground level. Pebbles, dirt, weeds. He pulls himself through by clutching at the ground, groaning as he squeezes through the narrow space. Blazing, blinding sunlight.*

Panting, he finally stands up. A three- or four-day beard. Ragged, disheveled, utterly spent.

Wider shot. The building he has escaped from is a three-story cinder-block warehouse or manufacturing site. The sign on the building reads: BARTHOLDI CASKET CO.

IZZY *begins hobbling away from the building. He begins to run.*

As IZZY *exits frame, we see the Statue of Liberty looming up in the distance.*

67. INT: DAY. PHILIP KLEINMAN'S APARTMENT. OFFICE SPACE.

A smallish, simple room: the office of a hard-working, independent producer. There are three movie posters hanging on the walls. The first one is The Incredible Shrinking Man. *The second:* Singin' in the Rain. *The third:* La Grande Illusion.

PHILIP

It's a disaster, the worst thing I've ever lived through. She just vanished into thin air. Twelve days of shooting, and on the thirteenth day, she doesn't show up. We had to shut down and send everyone home. The insurance company has three detectives looking for her, and not one of them has found a lead. Nothing. Not even a whiff.

Cut to:

IZZY, *shaved and dressed in clean clothes, is sitting in a chair on one side of* PHILIP's *desk.*

IZZY

(*Barely able to speak*) I should have been there with her. (*Beat*) I never should have waited.

PHILIP

(*After a moment*) To tell you the truth, I still have trouble believing what happened. The whole thing's like a dream . . . like she was never really there.

IZZY

(*As if drained of force*) Was she good?

PHILIP

Better than good. (*Beat*) She was extraordinary.

They sit in silence for a few moments, each one lost in his own thoughts. Eventually, IZZY tries to stand up. He is terribly weak, almost unable to move. He gets halfway out of his chair when his knees buckle and he begins to fall. He grabs hold of the desk to steady himself.

PHILIP rushes around from the other side and puts his arm around IZZY to prop him up.

PHILIP

Are you okay?

IZZY

(*Holding on to the desk; trying to maintain his balance; very weak*) Yeah. (*Beat*) Yeah, I'm okay.

PHILIP

Do you want a doctor?

IZZY

No. I'm all right.

With PHILIP's *arm still around him, they advance toward the door. To one side of the doorway, pushed against the wall, there is a small table with a pile of videocassettes on it.*

PHILIP

(*Seeing the cassettes*) I almost forgot. You should have one of these. (*Hands a cassette to* IZZY, *who doesn't say anything*) This is what there is. The editor put together a rough cut of the scenes we shot, and I had them transferred to video. Keep it.

IZZY

(*Taking the video. After a moment; softly*) Thank you.

PHILIP

(*Studying* IZZY) Go home, Izzy. You don't look so good. You need some rest. (*Beat*) Okay?

IZZY

(*Looking down; barely audible*) Okay.

PHILIP

I'll call you if I hear anything.

68. INT: DAY. WHITE HORSE TAVERN.

IZZY *is sitting in the back room of the tavern with* DAVE REILLY *and* TYRONE LORD, *two members of Katmandu. (We have seen them earlier: in scenes 1 and 3.)*

The room is nearly empty. Afternoon light slants through the window. They are sitting in a booth: IZZY *on one side;* DAVE *and* TYRONE *on the other. All three have drinks in front of them. It appears that they have been there for some time.*

IZZY

(*With more vigor than in the previous scene*) You don't believe me, do you?

DAVE *and* TYRONE *exchange a brief private glance, as if to say they don't.*

DAVE

Sure, we believe you, Izzy. Why shouldn't we believe you?

TYRONE

(*Nods*) Definitely.

IZZY *watches them closely. He understands that they are humoring him.*

IZZY

(*Leaning forward*) Tell me. Am I a stone or a tree?

DAVE

Huh?

IZZY

Just answer the question. Am I a stone or a tree?

DAVE and TYRONE ponder for a moment, trying to play along. They answer simultaneously.

> DAVE

A stone.

> TYRONE

A tree.

DAVE and TYRONE exchange another glance. DAVE shrugs.

> IZZY

(*Not giving up*) Am I a dog or a bird?

> TYRONE

(*More into it than Dave*) You're both, man. You're a dog with wings.

DAVE smiles.

> IZZY

(*More intense, taking hold of* TYRONE's *hand; an arm-wrestling position*) Am I a good person or a bad person?

> DAVE

(*Interrupting*) Cut it out, Izzy. You're going to drive yourself crazy.

> TYRONE

(*Taking* IZZY's *question seriously. Still gripping his hand; looking him straight in the eye*) You're good, Iz. You're good with some bad stuff mixed in. Just like everyone else.

> IZZY

(*Letting go of* TYRONE's *hand. Slumps back in his seat. After a moment: very quietly, as if talking to himself*) Am I here . . . or not here?

Again, DAVE and TYRONE exchange a meaningful glance. The camera turns back on IZZY. *He is looking down.*

DAVE (*off*)

What difference does it make? Life is just an illusion anyway—right?
(*Beat*) Don't worry about it.

Fade out. Music begins to play: slow, deep, sonorous. A piece for full orchestra.

69. INT: NIGHT. IZZY'S APARTMENT. THE BEDROOM.

The music continues.

The scene begins with a close-up of IZZY's face. He is sitting on the floor, his back leaning against the bed, watching television. No sound—only the music, which slowly and steadily builds in fullness and volume during the course of the scene.

It is a videotape of Pandora's Box. *The scene, which plays in silence throughout, shows LULU walking across her bedroom in her wedding dress. The camera never leaves LULU during the scene. Various close-ups of her face. She is at the height of her beauty here, and she gives off an air of innocent, almost virginal joy.*

Intercut between the video and IZZY's face. He becomes increasingly anguished as the film continues. Eventually, he begins to cry. A bit later, he closes his eyes, unable to watch anymore. With his eyes still closed, cut to:

70. INT: NIGHT. THE JAZZ CLUB FROM SCENE 3.

The music continues, the volume steadily building.

Another shot of IZZY's face, his eyes still closed. The camera backs up. We see him lying on the floor of the jazz club from scene 3. The shooting has just taken place. The camera continues to back away from him. We see the confusion of the frightened, stampeding crowd. TYRONE tends to IZZY, clamping his palms over the wound. Blood seeps out onto his hands. With his head, he gestures frantically for help. Cut to:

71. EXT: NIGHT. THE STREET IN FRONT OF THE JAZZ CLUB.

The music continues.

With a large crowd of gawkers milling around the entrance of the club, IZZY is carried out of the building on a stretcher by two paramedics. We see the back doors of the ambulance slam shut.

72. INT/EXT: NIGHT. INSIDE THE AMBULANCE/THE STREET.

The music continues.

As the ambulance speeds down the street, we see IZZY lying on his back, attended to by the two paramedics. An IV tube is in his arm. A wire connects his body to a monitor. Cut to:

Outside. We see CELIA walking down the street, alone. She is perhaps fifty feet ahead of the ambulance. She turns back at the sound of the siren. Cut to:

Inside the ambulance. The monitor is registering a flat line. IZZY's heart has stopped beating. One of the paramedics shakes his head.

FIRST PARAMEDIC
He's gone. We lost him.

SECOND PARAMEDIC
(*To the driver up front*) Cut the siren, Frank. The guy's dead.

Cut to:

Outside. CELIA has stopped walking. She is watching the ambulance, which has almost caught up to her. The siren is turned off: a series of strange, stuttering, popping sounds; the noise diminishes to silence. The ambulance slows down. CELIA, understanding that the person inside is dead, makes the sign of

138

the cross on her chest with her right hand. She stands there watching the ambulance as it passes by and continues on its way through the traffic. A close-up of her face. A long moment.

The screen goes black. A few moments of total silence. The credits come on, accompanied by a female voice performing "Singin' in the Rain."

The Making of

lulu on the bridge

Paul Auster
writer and director

Rebecca Prime: Three years ago, when you were working on the postproduction of *Smoke* and *Blue in the Face,* you did an interview with Annette Insdorf, and the last question she asked you was, "Now that you've caught the bug, do you have any desire to direct again?" You answered her, "No, I can't say that I do." Obviously, you've had a change of heart. Any particular reason?

Paul Auster: I guess it's dangerous to talk about the future, isn't it? The idea for *Lulu* actually came to me around that time, while I was still working on those films. I saw the story as a movie. And because I was feeling burned out by movies just then—postproduction on *Smoke* and *Blue in the Face* dragged on for almost a year—I did everything I could to resist it. But the story kept coming back to me, kept demanding that I do something about it, and eventually I gave in to the impulse. And when I did, I made a fatal mistake.

RP: How so?

PA: I decided to write it as a novel. If the story was good, I said to myself, then it didn't matter how I told it. Book, film, it didn't matter. The heart of the story would burn through no matter what form it took. So I sat down and started writing—and six or seven months later, when I stood up and examined what I had done so far, I realized it was no good. It didn't work. It was a dramatic story, not a narrative story, and it needed to be seen, not just read.

RP: Why?

PA: Because of the stone, to begin with. Because of the film inside the story. Because of the dreamlike structure of events. A whole host of reasons.

RP: And so you went back and started over again . . .

PA: Not right away. I thought the project was dead, and I turned my attention to other things. A year went by, maybe a year and a half, but the story never really left me. When I finally understood that it was something I needed to do, I took a deep breath and started again. But this time I stuck to my original conception and wrote it as a screenplay. So much for trying to force things. I learned a lot from that blunder.

RP: Still, even though you wrote it as a film, the story feels more like a novel than most films one sees. Like one of *your* novels, actually.

PA: Well, habits die hard, as Izzy says at one point. But the fact was that I felt all along that *Lulu* was a continuation of my work, that it's of a piece with everything else I've done.

RP: Most films seem to set out to tell one thing, and they usually proceed in a linear fashion. With *Lulu on the Bridge,* the story works on several different levels at once.

PA: That's what makes it so difficult to talk about. There are a number of threads running through the story, and by the time you come to the end, they're so tangled up with one another, you can't pull one out without disturbing all the others. The most important thing, though, is that at bottom it's a very emotional story, a story about deep and powerful feelings. It's not a puzzle, not some code to be cracked, and you don't have to "understand" it in a rational way to feel the force of the emotions.

RP: Let's talk about the "dreamlike structure of events" you mentioned earlier.

PA: On one level, it's all very simple. A man gets shot, and in the last hour before his death, he dreams another life for himself. The content of that dream is provided by a number of random elements that appear to him just before and after the shooting. A wall of photographs in a men's room featuring women's faces—mostly the faces of movie stars—and a chunk of plaster that falls from the ceiling. Everything follows from those elements: the magic blue stone, the young woman he falls in love with, the fact that she's an actress and lands a role in a film, the title of that film, the director of that film, and so on. That's one way of reading the story—the framework, so to speak. But that's hardly the most interesting way of looking at it. It gives the film some plausibility, I suppose, but it doesn't take the magic into account. And if you forget the magic, you don't have much of anything.

RP: Can you elaborate?

PA: Because, on another level, all these things really happen. I firmly believe that Izzy lives through the events in the story, that the dream is not just some empty fantasy. When he dies at the end, he's a different man than he was at the beginning. He's managed to redeem himself, somehow. If not, how else to account for Celia's presence on the street at the end? It's as if she has lived through the story, too. The ambulance passes, and even though she can't possibly know who is inside, she does, it's as if she does. She feels a connection, she's moved, she's touched by grief—understanding that the person in the ambulance has just died. As far as I'm concerned, the whole film comes together in that final shot. The magic isn't just simply a dream. It's real, and it carries all the emotions of reality.

RP: In other words, you believe in the impossible.

PA: We all do. Whether we know it or not, our lives would make no sense if we didn't. . . . Think of something like *A Midsummer Night's Dream*. Elves and fairies prancing through the woods. Sprinkle pixie dust in a man's eyes, and he falls in love. It's impossible, yes, but that doesn't mean it isn't real, that it isn't true to life. Love is magic, after all, isn't it? No one understands what it is, no one can explain it. Pixie dust is as good an explanation as any other, it seems to me. And so is the blue stone—the thing that brings Izzy and Celia together. Just because a story is told "realistically" doesn't make it realistic. And just because a story is told fancifully doesn't make it far-fetched. In the end, metaphor might be the best way of getting at the truth.

RP: *Lulu on the Bridge* operates on a metaphorical level, but it is also grounded in reality.

PA: Well, you can never stray too far from the world of ordinary things. If you do, you slip into allegory, and allegory doesn't interest me at all. Two or three years ago, Peter Brook did an interview in the *New York Times,* and he said something that made an enormous impression on me. "In all my work," he said, "I try to combine the closeness of the everyday with the distance of myth. Because, without the closeness you can't be moved, and without the distance you can't be amazed." A brilliant formulation, no? *Lulu on the Bridge* is that kind of double work, I think. At least I hope it is.

RP: When all is said and done, *Lulu* could probably be described as a love story, couldn't it? That seems to be the heart of the film, at least for me. What happens between Izzy and Celia.

PA: Yes, I think you're right. Izzy is a man who's led a less than noble life. He's selfish, quick-tempered, incapable of loving anyone. He's cut off from his family, and his marriage to Hannah—a beautiful, good-hearted young woman—ended after just a few years. Probably because he couldn't keep his hands off of other women. Then he's shot, and in the delirium of his final moments, he conjures up a great and overpowering love. In doing so, he reinvents who he is, becomes better, discovers what is best inside him. It's a big love, of course. A love so big he's actually willing to die for it.

RP: Izzy is willing to die for Celia, but Celia also sacrifices herself for Izzy.

PA: Precisely. It works both ways. Celia jumps off the bridge and disappears. You think that might be the end of her. Then Izzy dies, and just as he is pronounced dead in the ambulance, we see Celia again, walking down the street. It's as if his death has resurrected her, as if he's died in order to give her another chance at life.

RP: Tell me about the stone. It's probably the strangest element in the story, and yet the odd thing is that everyone seems to accept it. I've attended several screenings of the film, and not once has anyone questioned it or been confused by it.

PA: To tell the truth, I don't really understand what the stone is. I have ideas about it, of course, many feelings, many thoughts, but nothing definitive.

RP: Each person finds his or her own meaning in it . . .

PA: Yes. It becomes more powerful that way, I think. The less fixed, the more pregnant with possibilities. . . . When I first wrote the story, I suppose I thought of the stone as some kind of mysterious, all-encompassing life force—the glue that connects one thing to another, that binds people together, the unknowable something that makes love possible. Later on, when we filmed the scene of Izzy pulling the stone out of the box, I began to have another idea about it. The way Harvey played it, it began to feel to me as if the stone were Izzy's soul, as if we were watching a man discover himself for the first time. He reacts with fear and confusion; he's thrown into a panic. It's only the next day, when he meets Celia, that he understands what's happened. You find your essence only in relation to others. That's the great paradox. You don't take hold of yourself until you're willing to give it away. In other words, you don't become who you are until you're capable of loving someone else.

RP: The stone is one of the elements in the film that clues the viewer to the fact that you can't read the film as a straightforward narrative, that we're clearly in some sort of altered universe. At the same time, it has a very straightforward narrative function. It's the prime mover in what could be called the "thriller" aspect of the story. What compelled you to make use of this genre?

PA: Because it seemed right, it felt right. Thrillers are very much like dreams. When you strip away the surface details, they begin to function as metaphors of our unconscious. People without faces pursuing you through dark, abandoned streets. Men hanging from the edges of buildings. Fear and danger, risk, the contingencies of life and death.

RP: With *Lulu,* how would you describe the thriller aspect of the plot?

PA: It's fairly rudimentary. Dr. Van Horn is associated with the group that developed the magic stone. Various scoundrels representing other groups are trying to gain possession of this priceless object. Stanley Mar would be one. The three thugs who assault Izzy would be another. They lock him up, thinking he knows where the stone is. Then Van Horn's group tracks down this other group and eliminates them. Van Horn then begins to interrogate Izzy.

RP: But he's interested in more than just the stone, isn't he?

PA: Of course he is. He's interested in Izzy's soul. Van Horn isn't at all what he first appears to be. He's an interrogating angel. He's the figure standing between Izzy and the gates of death. His job is to find out who Izzy is.

RP: In their last conversation, when Izzy refuses to reveal that he knows Celia Burns, Van Horn storms out in a fit of anger. Why?

PA: Because he wants the stone, and he understands that Izzy isn't going to help him. At the same time, I see his anger as a test. He wants to know if Izzy will buckle under the pressure or try to protect the person he loves. Izzy stands firm, and even though Van Horn doesn't get what he seems to want, in the end this might be an even more satisfying outcome for him. Remember, he doesn't rush out. He turns at the last moment and says to Izzy, "May God have mercy on your soul." And he means it. There's tremendous ambiguity in that line, of course, but it also represents a spontaneous outburst of compassion.

RP: And then there's Celia—what might be called the "feminine" side of the movie. In some sense, she's everything Izzy is not.

PA: Her most important quality, I think, is vitality. Celia is *alive.* She's generous, she's fetching, she's desirable—the kind of young woman every man can fall in love with. At the same time, she's not a pushover. She's not some simpering cutie-pie. She has opinions, she's capable of anger, she's willing to stand up for herself.

RP: And she's also an actress. I was particularly struck by the line she says to Izzy about playing a prostitute: "I really liked doing that scene." It gives us a glimpse into how she might be capable of playing Lulu.

PA: Yes. It's a jocular, offhanded kind of line, but it does establish an important link. It's a little fulcrum that connects Celia to Lulu.

RP: Celia is a flesh-and-blood character, but at the same time there's a fascination with female archetypes in the film. Just under the surface, the story seems to be making constant references to myth. When Celia looks up at Izzy after she's taken hold of the stone for the first time and says, "Come on, don't be afraid, it's the best thing, it really is," you feel this is just the kind of thing Eve might have said to Adam in the Garden of Eden. When Izzy opens the three boxes and finds the stone in the last one, you can't help but think of Pandora's box.

PA: All the images in the story are connected; everything bounces off of everything else. To a large degree, the film is about how men invent women. It begins with the very first shot—when we see that wall of photographs of women's faces. All those movie stars! I'm intrigued by the fact that for most of this century images of beautiful women have been projected on screens and have fed the fantasies of men all over the world. That's probably why movie stars were invented. To feed dreams. Izzy invents a new life for himself through the medium of a picture. There's Mira Sorvino's face on the wall—and the movie begins. In a way, it duplicates what we all experience when we watch movies. We walk into a dark place and leave the world behind. We enter the realm of make-believe.

RP: Why Lulu and *Pandora's Box*? What exactly were you trying to do by introducing that element into the story?

PA: It pushes the dream farther, throws Celia from one end of her femininity to the other. From good girl to bad girl. It's Izzy's dream, after all, and in some way you can see Lulu as a female version of who Izzy used to be.

RP: I see what you mean when you say the "everything bounces off everything else."

PA: That's why I was so gripped by the Lulu story. Lulu is a completely amoral, infantile creature, a person without compassion. Men lose their minds over her. She doesn't intend to hurt anybody, but one by one all her lovers are driven to suicide, insanity, debasement— every horror you can imagine. Lulu is a blank slate, and men project their desires onto her. They invent her. Just as men invent the women they see in movies. The Lulu plays were written before the invention of movies, but Lulu is a movie star. She's the first movie star in history.

RP: How did you go about adapting the Lulu material?

PA: I went back to Wedekind's two plays, *Earth Spirit* and *Pandora's Box*. I greatly admire Pabst's film, particularly Louise Brooks's performance, but I didn't make much use of it when writing the screenplay, and I certainly didn't want to refer to it in the film. The two plays tell a continuous story, and they add up to nine long acts. Obviously, I couldn't deal with all that. The most I could do was suggest the arc of Lulu's life, and I tried to achieve that by concentrating on what I felt were a few of the most interesting and pertinent scenes. I also decided not to do it as a period piece, to modernize the details, the settings, and so on. The plays are a hundred years old now, and there's so much dreadful writing in them, so much that creaks and grates, there seemed to be no point in trying to restage them as they were written. In the first scene, I changed the painter Schwarz into the photographer Black. The Pierrot costume became a Charlie Chaplin costume. All in the spirit of the original—but different. In the dressing-room scene, I changed the musical revue into a rock and roll performance. That kind of thing. It's never a word-for-word translation, but at the same time I tried not to stray too far from the gist of Wedekind's dialogue.

RP: Once you started writing the screenplay, were you also planning to direct the film yourself?

PA: Not at first. The original idea was for Wim Wenders to direct it. Wim and I have been friends for a long time now, and we've always talked about doing a project together. For a while, it looked as though *Lulu* would be that project. We even went so far as to have a number of conversations about the story, and when I sent him the finished screenplay, he was very happy with it. I assumed that would be the end of my involvement with the film, that the torch had been passed, so to speak. Then, just a few days later, a funny thing happened. Wim was interviewed by a journalist, and at one point she said to him, "Mr. Wenders, do you realize that the past four or five movies you've made have all been about making movies?" The question caught him by surprise. As a matter of fact, he hadn't been aware of it. *Lulu on the Bridge,* of course, is yet another movie with a movie inside the movie, and Wim called me up the next morning to say that he was suddenly feeling worried. Was that his destiny—to be a filmmaker who could only make films about films? He wasn't backing out of the project, but he wanted to think it over for a while before committing himself. Was that okay? Of course it was okay. So I hung up the phone and realized that the film no longer had a director.

RP: How could you be sure?

PA: Making a movie is such a difficult, exhausting process, you can't go into it with anything less than total enthusiasm. The slightest doubt, the smallest flicker of uncertainty, and you're sunk. If Wim was wobbling about it, then my feeling was that he probably shouldn't do it. . . . He was going to call me back with his decision the following week, and in the meantime I started thinking about who else should do it, who else *could* do it. No names jumped out at me. The script is so strange, I suppose, so particular to me and my own private universe, that I couldn't think of anyone whose sensibility would be compatible with the material. That was when it occurred to me that perhaps I should do it myself. It was my story, after all, and why not see the thing through to the end? At least it would be made exactly the way I wanted it to be made—for better or for worse. So I wrote Wim a fax saying that if he decided not to direct the film, I was inclined to do it myself. I sent the letter through the machine, and one minute later the telephone rang. It was Wim. "I just tore up a letter I was going to fax to you," he said, "trying to persuade you to direct the movie yourself." And that was that. Without really intending to work in the movies again, not only had I written another screenplay, but now I was going to direct as well.

RP: And you weren't scared?

PA: No, not really. I had spent two years working on *Smoke* and *Blue in the Face* and had a very clear idea of what I was getting myself into. No one twisted my arm to do it. It was a decision I made on my own, which means that somewhere, deep down, I had probably had a real hankering to do it.

RP: You finished writing the script in early February 1997. Now, almost exactly a year later, you're in postproduction. How did it happen so fast?

PA: Two words: Peter Newman. Peter was the producer of both *Smoke* and *Blue in the Face,* and once we started working together, we became great friends. I can't say enough good things about this man. His integrity, his optimism, his sense of humor, his resilience. When I told him about this new project that I wanted to do, he simply went out and raised the money. In record time. It only took about two months.

RP: Peter Newman was also responsible for one of the scenes in the film, wasn't he?

PA: I'm not sure he'd want me to talk about it—but yes, he was. The airplane story that Philip Kleinman tells at the dinner party early in the film came directly from Peter. It's a true story, something that really happened to him. I know it's rather disgusting, and more than a little disturbing, but the fact was that I was very impressed when Peter told it to me—for what it revealed about his moral qualities, his goodness as a human being. That's how it stands in the film: as a moral tale.

RP: How did you go about casting the film? Did you write the script with any specific actors in mind?

PA: Harvey Keitel. He was the only one. It's not that I set out to write a role for Harvey, but once I got into the story a bit, I began seeing him in my mind, and at a certain point it became inconceivable to think of Izzy without also thinking of Harvey.

RP: You'd worked together before, of course.

PA: Yes, and we'd both developed a great deal of respect for each other. It goes without saying that Harvey is a superb actor. But there's something more to it than that. The way he moves, the irresistible qualities of his face, his groundedness. It's as if Harvey embodies something that belongs to all of us, as if he *becomes* us when he's up on the screen. When he agreed to play Izzy, I knew that we were going to have an extraordinary time together. And we did. Working with him on this role was one of the best experiences of my life.

RP: Mira Sorvino plays Celia, but at an earlier stage in the project the part was supposedly offered to Juliette Binoche. Is that true?

PA: Yes. But that was very early, when Wim still thought he would be involved. Juliette was the actress he proposed, and she was interested. But then she won her Academy Award, and in all the uproar that followed, it became difficult for her to decide what to do next. So I moved on. It's not as though this kind of thing doesn't happen every day when you're trying to put together a movie. Early on, I formulated a little phrase to help me get through the inevitable disappointments and hard knocks ahead. "Every person and every thing is replaceable," I told myself, "except the script." I've repeated those words to myself a thousand times since then, and they've helped; they've more or less allowed me to keep my head screwed on straight.

RP: So you lost one Academy Award actress and got another. Not such a bad trade-off!

PA: The gods were smiling on me, there's no question about it. . . . It's such a difficult, complex role—in effect two roles, many roles—and only a very gifted actress could begin to do it justice. I had worked with Mira for one day on *Blue in the Face* and had been impressed with her intelligence and talent. She has a fierce commitment to getting things right, and you can't learn that kind of attitude—it's who you are. Last spring, we both happened to wind up on the jury at Cannes. We saw each other every day for two weeks and got to know each other better, to become friends. When it finally became clear to me that Juliette wasn't going to be in the film, I didn't hesitate to ask Mira. It turned out to be my luckiest stroke, the smartest move I made. I knew she was going to be good, but I had no idea she had it in her to reach the heights she did, to touch such deep emotional chords. Mira is a very brave person, a girl with guts. And yet she's also immensely fragile. Her pores are open to the world, and she feels everything, registers everything happening in the air around her. Like a tuning fork. It's rare to find this combination of strength and sensitivity in one person. Mix that in with a keen mind and a heavy

dose of natural talent, and you really have yourself something. And Mira is really something. I loved the whole adventure of working with her.

RP: What about the other actors? There are at least thirty speaking parts in the film.

PA: In many cases, I approached actors I had worked with before. Giancarlo Esposito, Jared Harris, Victor Argo, Peggy Gormley, and Harold Perrineau had all been involved with *Smoke* and *Blue in the Face*. It was a great advantage to be able to turn to them, because I knew that I could trust them—not just as actors, but as people. Gina Gershon is a close friend of one of my wife's sisters, and we've known each other for years. Mandy Patinkin had played the lead in *The Music of Chance*. Vanessa Redgrave was also a friend. And even Stockard Channing, who couldn't be in the film, did me a little favor a couple of weeks ago when she came in and recorded the phone message that Celia receives from her agent telling her she's been given the part. You might not see Stockard in the film, but you hear her voice!

RP: Do-it-yourself casting.

PA: To a small degree. All the other actors came through Heidi Levitt, who was in charge of casting. Auditions, video reels, telephone calls, nail-biting decisions.

RP: What about Willem Dafoe?

PA: That was a different story, a completely different story. Originally, Dr. Van Horn was called Dr. Singh, and the role was going to be played by Salman Rushdie. Salman is another friend, a very good friend, but also—believe it or not—a wonderfully able actor. I asked him to be in the movie just after I finished the script, and he accepted. We were both very excited about it.

RP: What were your reasons for thinking of him?

PA: First of all, as a recognizable figure, his presence would have reinforced the constant overlapping of dream and reality in the film. A man who has been forced into hiding through terrible, tragic circumstances suddenly appears as a man in charge of interrogating someone who is being held against his will. The captive made captor. It was my little way of trying to turn the tables on the world. I wanted to make a gesture in Salman's defense, to reinvent reality just enough for it to be possible to have Salman Rushdie appear in the film—not as himself, but as an imaginary character. Finally—and most important of all—I knew that he would give an excellent performance.

RP: Why didn't it happen?

PA: Fear, mostly. And bad planning on my part, bad planning all around. I've spent so much time with him, have been in so many public places with him—restaurants, theaters, the streets of New York— that I forget that most people think of him as a walking time bomb, that if they get anywhere near him, they're likely to be blown to bits. Nine years have gone by since the *fatwa* was declared, and he's still, mercifully, very much with us, but his name seems to trigger off an irrational panic in many people, and a certain percentage of the crew wanted extra security guarantees if he was going to appear in the film. The cost of doing such a thing would have been prohibitive, and eventually I had to abandon the idea. I fought tooth and nail to make it happen, but it didn't. It was a tremendous disappointment to me. I consider it a personal defeat, a moral defeat.

RP: The film was already in production at that point, wasn't it?

PA: We were in our sixth week, and those scenes were scheduled for the eighth week—the last days of shooting in New York.

RP: It didn't leave you much time, did it?

PA: Our backs were right up against the wall. I thought the movie would have to shut down, that we wouldn't be able to finish. It was an awful period, let me tell you.

RP: So Willem stepped in—literally at the last minute.

PA: The very last minute. He received the script on a Sunday, accepted the role on Monday, and when he showed up for a rehearsal with me and Harvey the following Sunday, he had his part down cold. He knew every line perfectly. The next day, Monday, we filmed his first scene. Can you imagine? He's positively brilliant in the role, and he prepared the whole thing in a week. Willem saved the movie. He stepped in and single-handedly rescued us all. It was heroic what he did, and I'm so grateful to him, so deeply in his debt, that I can hardly think about it without getting a little weak in the knees.

RP: You learn to roll with the punches, don't you?

PA: You don't have any choice. Things are going to go wrong. You never know when, and you never know how, but you can be sure it will happen when you're least expecting it. That's why you need to have a good group of people around you, people you can depend on. I was very lucky in that regard. I had a game and cooperative cast, a

valiant first assistant director—Bobby Warren—and the people I hired to head the various departments all broke their backs to make the film work. It's not just a matter of knowledge and technical skill. It comes down to character and soul, the way you live your life. Not losing your temper, keeping your sense of humor under trying circumstances, respecting the efforts of others, taking pride in your own work. All the old-fashioned virtues. I can't emphasize how important these things are on a movie set. You have to create a good environment for people to work in, to establish a sense of solidarity. If that doesn't happen, the whole thing can go to hell in about two seconds.

RP: How did you go about choosing the different creative department heads—production designer, costume designer, director of photography, and so on?

PA: I suppose it was similar to the casting. A combination of people I had worked with before, friends, and absolute strangers.

RP: Kalina Ivanov, the production designer, was a *Smoke* and *Blue in the Face* veteran.

PA: Exactly. We had remained friends in the interim, and the truth is that it never occurred to me to ask anyone else to handle the job. Kalina is more than just a designer. She's a real filmmaker, a participant in the whole process. And she also has one of the most energetic, ebullient personalities I've ever encountered—with this great big Bulgarian laugh and a wicked sense of humor. You need people like Kalina with you—people who love challenges, who never take no for an answer, who walk through fire if that's what it takes to get the job done.

RP: And Adelle Lutz, the costume designer?

PA: Known to everyone as Bonny. A friend. But also someone whose work I had admired for a long time. Costumes are an important element in *Lulu,* especially in the *Pandora's Box* sections, and I needed someone with tremendous flair and imagination, a person with original ideas. Just as important, I knew that Bonny was a grown-up and would be able to handle the pressures of the job—which were clearly going to be enormous.

RP: Why enormous?

PA: Because there were so many characters to dress and design costumes for—and so few dollars and days to do it in. A lesser person would have cracked up and jumped out the window.

RP: Surely you exaggerate.

PA: Well, maybe a little—but not as much as you might think. The whole film had to operate on a very restricted budget, but the wardrobe department got the worst of it, I think. One example stands out very vividly in my mind. In the original script, the last segment from *Pandora's Box*—the one that Izzy watches in silence on his VCR—was an elaborate wedding scene that had at least fifty actors and actresses in it. It was supposed to be from an earlier moment in the story, and therefore everyone who had died later on—Peter Shine, Candy, and Lulu—would be seen alive again, in the pink of health, happy, resurrected, with a resplendent Lulu floating among them in her wedding dress. It would have been beautiful, but the hard fact was that we couldn't afford to do it. The extras were one thing, but once Bonny toted up the costs of dressing fifty actors in evening clothes, the expense proved to be too great. At first, I thought about reducing the number of guests at the party, but as I continued to whittle down the list, this compromise began to look rather dismal. What saved the scene was the extraordinary dress that Bonny designed for Mira—the one with the peacock feathers. It was so striking, so sublime, that it allowed me to rethink the scene and do it with no guests at all. Just Lulu alone in her bedroom, right after she's climbed into the dress. It turned out well, I think, and visually it's one of the strongest scenes in the film. But it was motivated by desperation. Without Bonny, I would have been lost.

RP: And what about Alik Sakharov, the director of photography? How did you decide to work with him?

PA: Because I knew the schedule was going to be very intense and grueling, I wanted to hire someone who was rather young—a person with a lot of physical stamina, who still had something to prove to the world. I interviewed quite a few people, some of them very well known. At first, Alik wasn't even on the list. But then Kalina called me up and urged me to meet with him. She talked about his work so enthusiastically, I couldn't resist—even though I was on the verge of hiring someone else. It was a sunny day in late spring, I remember, and Alik came to my house. Not only had he read the script thoroughly, and not only did he understand it and admire it, but he had written out extensive notes about how he would go about filming it. I myself had very definite ideas about how I wanted the film to look and had already thought about how many of the scenes should be shot. For the first thirty or forty minutes, I didn't say much. When you're interviewing someone, it's always more important to hear what

the other person has to say. So I asked Alik how he would approach this scene, and then that scene, and then this other scene, and after a while it was as if I were listening to my own thoughts. Shot for shot, look for look, he had almost the same idea about the film that I did.

RP: What kinds of preparations did you and Alik make before filming began?

PA: We worked for weeks, just the two of us, all through the late summer and early fall, talking through every scene again and again, making up shot lists, analyzing the story in visual terms. That was the foundation of the film. Everything grew from those early conversations. Not only did we develop a plan that we both believed in, but we learned to trust each other, to depend on each other's insights and judgments. By the time filming began, we were comrades, partners in a single enterprise. We worked together in a state of tremendous harmony, and I can't tell you how important that was to me on the set. Alik was a rock of dependability, and I could always count on him, could always get my ideas through to him. He's a man of great dignity and depth of soul, and he has the endurance of a marathon runner. We were on the set for at least twelve hours every day, would go to the Technicolor lab in midtown for dailies every night, and often had to squeeze in time to scout new locations before, between, or after the day's work. And from start to finish, Alik kept going at full tilt. He was my closest collaborator on the film, the one person who was with me every step of the way.

RP: What was it like working with the actors?

PA: That's the fun part, the best part of the job. Four years ago, when Wayne [Wang] and I started rehearsing for *Smoke,* I discovered that I felt naturally connected to actors, that I had an innate sympathy for what they do. A startling discovery to make so late in life, no? But when you stop and think about it, there's a definite affinity between acting and writing novels. In both cases, the object of the work is to bring imaginary beings to life, to take something that doesn't exist and make it real, make it believable. A writer does it with his pen, and an actor does it with his body, but they're both trying to achieve the same thing. In writing my books, I always have the feeling that I'm inside my characters, that I inhabit them, that I actually become them. Actors feel the same way about what they do, and because of that I don't have any trouble understanding what they say to me. Nor do they seem to have any trouble understanding what I say to them.

RP: As a director, you're part of a collaborative process. Did you miss the creative control you have as a writer?

PA: When I was a kid, I was very involved in sports. I played on a lot of teams—baseball teams, basketball teams, football teams—and until I was well into high school, it was probably the biggest thing in my life. Then I grew up, and for the next twenty-five years or so I spent most of my time alone, sitting in a room with a pen in my hand. You have to enjoy being alone to do that, and I do enjoy being alone, but that doesn't mean I don't enjoy working with other people, too. When I began collaborating with Wayne on our two movies, it

brought back memories of playing on those sports teams as a kid, and I realized that I had missed it, that I was glad to be participating in a group effort again. Yes, as a writer you have total control over what you're doing, and as a filmmaker you don't. But that's like saying oranges taste like oranges, and apples taste like apples. The two experiences are entirely different. When you write a book, you have all the time in the world. If you make a mistake, nobody sees you make it. You can just cross out the sentence and start over again. You can throw out a week's work, a month's work, and nobody cares. On a film set, you don't have that luxury. It's do or die every day. You have to accomplish your work on time, and you don't get a second chance. At least not with a tightly budgeted film like ours. So, needless to say, things can get pretty nerve-racking at times. But that doesn't mean they aren't enjoyable. When things go well, when everyone is doing his or her job the way it's supposed to be done and you pull off the thing you've set out to do, it becomes a beautiful experience, a deeply satisfying thing. I think that's why people get addicted to working in movies—the grips, the gaffers, the camera team, the prop men, the sound people, everyone. They work terribly hard, the hours are long, and no one gets rich, but every day is different from the day before. That's what keeps them at it: the adventure of it, the uncertainty, the fact that no one knows what's going to happen next.

RP: Did you find that the *imaginative* process involved in directing differs significantly from the one involved in writing?

PA: Not as much as you might think. The outward circumstances are utterly different, of course—one person sitting alone in a room as opposed to dozens of people on a noisy set—but at bottom you're trying to accomplish the same thing: to tell a story. *Lulu* was my script; it wasn't as if I was directing someone else's work. And I tried to use all the tools at my disposal to tell that story as well as I could: the actors, the camera, the lights, the locations, the sets, the costumes, and so on. Those elements create the syntax of the story. There were times when I thought: the camera is the ink, the lighting setups are punctuation marks, the props are adjectives, the actors' gestures are verbs. Very strange. But standing there on the set every day with the crew, I somehow felt that they were creating the story with me—with me and for me. It was as if they were all inside my head with me.

RP: Earlier, you talked about things going wrong on the set. Can you give me an example of what you meant?

PA: I could give you dozens of examples. Some big, some small. A lighting setup that short-circuited at the worst possible moment. A prop gun that kept misfiring. A dress that tore. All the usual mishaps. Once, I even ruined a take myself by laughing too hard. Jared Harris was doing something so funny, I just couldn't control myself any-more. . . . The incident I learned the most from, though, would have to be something that happened in the second or third week of shoot-ing. During preproduction, I had had several meetings with Jeff Mazzola, the prop master, and we had made a thorough list of all the things that would have to be on hand for every scene in the film. Jeff was an integral part of what we did every day, and beyond being a pleasant person to be around, he brought a lot of intelligence and enthusiasm to his work. He was the one who helped me design the stone that Izzy finds in the briefcase. He was the one who worked out the pie-in-the-face scene with me—and actually threw the pie at Mira. He was the one who drove the ambulance in the last scene. I mention these things so you'll have an idea of how closely we worked together. Anyway, for the scene in which Celia says good-bye to Izzy and drives off to the airport, we needed a black town car. I had specif-ically told Jeff that I wanted a car that had a back window that went all the way down—so that Celia would be able to lean out and blow Izzy a kiss as the car drove away. Most cars these days have windows that go only halfway down, and Jeff had given precise instructions to the car rental place that we needed an older-model car. So, the day arrives when we're supposed to shoot the scene, and the car shows up on the set. There was an establishing shot we had to do—the car parked in front of Celia's building—and since Harvey and Mira were still in the hair-and-makeup trailer getting ready for their first scene together, I figured we could knock off the establishing shot first, which would help us save time for more important things later in the day. Just to make sure, though, I told Jeff that we should check to see if the window went all the way down. No point in doing the shot if we had the wrong car, was there? And lo and behold, the window went only halfway down. I was furious. We were working on a very tight schedule, and I knew this little blunder was going to cost us precious time and money. What could I do? I couldn't very well turn on Jeff and start blaming him. It wasn't his fault. He had ordered the right car, and I wasn't about to criticize him for not doing his job. He *had* done his job. But still, you feel this anger surging up inside you, this horrible sense of frustration. Fortunately, Jeff was just as angry as I was. Even angrier, probably. He's so conscientious about his work, and he treated this screwup as an insult to his professional pride. That's when I learned an important lesson about being a director. You can actually live your anger through other people. Jeff called up the car rental place, and as I stood there next to him, listening to him scream and curse at the man responsible for the mistake, I began to feel much better. Jeff's anger was my anger, and because he could express it for me, I was able to stay calm. At least on the outside.

RP: Of all the hundreds of things that happened on the set, what moment are you proudest of?

PA: That's hard to say. In general, I'm proud of everything we did, of everyone's work. Even when we made mistakes, we always managed to fix them—so there's really nothing I look back on with any deep regret. But the proudest moment, I don't know. There's one *happy* moment that jumps out at me, however. I don't know why I think of this one now, but there it is. The pie-in-the-face scene. Maybe because I just mentioned it a few minutes ago. It's such a small part of the film, but it took a lot of careful preparation to get it right, and Mira was a great sport about it. We all had fun doing those four little video scenes. The horror movie, the pie-in-the-face, the nun praying over the dying child, and the hooker bit with Lou Reed in the bar. I gave Mira a different name for each of these parts, just to keep things amusing. The nun, I remember, was Sister Mira of the Perpetual

Performance. We probably had such a good time with these things because all the other work we did was so intense, so demanding, and these little clips gave us all a chance to relax a little, to play in a different key. Not just Mira and the other actors, but the crew as well. Anyway, I was very keen to do a pie-in-the-face gag. It's a lost art, an ancient turn that's vanished from films, and no one knows how to do it anymore. I asked a couple of older directors for advice, but they couldn't help me. "Just make it funny," one of them said. Yes, but how? So I had to sit down and figure it out for myself. The problem was that I didn't have any room for flubs. It had to be done perfectly on the first take. Otherwise, we would have needed three or four hours to set up the shot again, and we didn't have that kind of time to spend on such a small thing. If we got it wrong, the whole set would have to be redone, Mira's hair and makeup would have to be redone, and we couldn't afford to do that. The only solution was to devise a fail-proof technique.

RP: What did you use for the cream?

PA: Reddi Wip. We experimented with shaving cream, but it wasn't as good. Once everything was prepared and we'd gone through a couple of dry runs, I turned on some crazy Raymond Scott music to get everyone in the mood, and then I started giving instructions to Mira and David Byrne, who played the escort. The whole crew was watching anxiously, hoping it would work, and when it did, the whole place erupted in wild cheers and laughter. It was a wonderful moment. Not just for me, but for all of us. I remember saying to myself, "Good grief, I think I'm actually getting the hang of this job."

RP: Is it a job you'd like to do again?

PA: This is where we came in, isn't it?

RP: Not really. It's three years later, and you've just finished directing a film. Would you like to do it again?

PA: All things being equal, yes. But things are rarely equal, so I'm not going to speculate about the future anymore. The only thing I can say with any certainty is that I've poured myself into making *this* film, and I'm glad I had the chance to do it. It's been a big experience for me, and I'm never going to forget it.

February 22, 1998

Alik Sakharov
director of photography

Rebecca Prime: Were you familiar with Paul's writing before beginning this project?

Alik Sakharov: No. I was working on a film in South Carolina when Kalina Ivanov, who was the production designer, suggested I get acquainted with Paul's work, since he was going to be directing a film. When I got back to New York I went to Coliseum Books and bought everything they had by Paul. I liked what I read. I found his writing very inventive and at the same time very poignant. Although I didn't know him, I felt like he was a kindred spirit of sorts.

RP: Did the script for *Lulu* confirm this impression?

AS: Yes. I felt that the story was coming from a place I knew, a place I understood. I found the script incredibly poetic, and poetry in cinema is what I respond to most strongly. What I mean by poetry is transcendence, the ability of the image to take you from one place and put you in another. In what I consider poetic cinema, the framing is not as stylized, the lighting not as precise, the images not as geometrically exact. For example, if a tree is photographed from an angle that imitates the human perspective, the camera serves to put the viewer in the frame and in this way invokes an emotional response. The frame begins to look warmer, more accessible, not sterile or cold.

RP: So you responded to the story on an emotional level.

AS: Yes, but also on an intellectual one. I really liked the complexity of the film's infrastructure. There is a fine thread that unites certain scenes together, but many things are never fully explained. You can read the film as very linear and straightforward, but this leads you into trouble because the film operates on so many different levels. Once you understand the film's structure, you see that it is ultimately very simple, but it requires an intellectual process to arrive at this understanding. It has an open ending, really. The film is over, but you keep thinking about it, and that to me is a successful film.

RP: Did you find that you and Paul understood the film in similar terms?

AS: A cinematographer's job is to try to photograph the world the way the director sees it. You try to create and capture the images that he is carrying in his head, to interpret his thoughts visually. It was very evident from the start that Paul wrote the screenplay with a very lucid vision of the picture and of its development. When Paul speaks, he describes his ideas so clearly that you get it, just like that. From what I know of Tarkovsky, for instance, he was not able to communicate his ideas as successfully. I once saw a documentary about him and was very surprised to hear him speak to his cinematographer in vague terms: "You know, it's that feeling, it's like, you know, well, how should I say it . . ." He didn't make his point clearly. His meaning remained elusive. With Paul, what he means and what he wants to happen are right there in the words. So for me, it was very easy to interpret the information he gave me and to design the shot accordingly. There were times when he didn't know the exact cinematic terms, but all his ideas were so clear that it was easy to translate them into basic cinema lingo so that the crew could understand. Paul was also very receptive to other people's ideas.

Because I saw the film as profoundly human, I wanted to photograph it in a real, naturalistic style. I felt that it was important to construct the images extremely carefully so as to be as subtle as possible. They could be elegant, they could be beautiful, but I didn't want them to call attention to themselves and detract from the film. I was very glad that Paul saw the film in a similar way. Many times, I would quickly set up a shot to show Paul how I imagined it, and through his encouragement, he would let me know that he agreed. When we looked at each other, it would be with such a feeling of cooperative understanding.

RP: Were your working styles similarly in sync?

AS: I like to know in advance what we plan to do rather than figuring it out on the day we shoot the scene. There's nothing wrong with amending your ideas on set, as long as you have a base plan to begin with. Especially when working on projects with a tight schedule, arriving on set raw is just a bad idea. So personally, I wanted to visualize the scenes long before we would shoot them. When I realized that Paul also preferred to plan things out ahead of time, I felt so at rest.

I think that the fact that we began production as well-prepared as we were also helped to generate the calm, pleasant atmosphere we had on set. I often talk to people who worked on the crew as day players, and they tell me that ours was one of the friendliest, most efficient sets they had ever worked on. I know how disorganized and crazy film sets can be, so it seems we must have done something right!

RP: But even with the best planning, theory and practice can often turn out to be quite different things. Would you say this was true in the case of *Lulu?*

AS: There was a moment when, theoretically, we had mapped out the entire structure of the film, and we all felt very happy with it. We knew how certain scenes would end and how others would begin, and in this way had been able to develop a distinct sense of the film's visual structure. The way we approached transforming this theory into practice was to break down the scenes into a shot list based on our abstract sense of the locations. When we started narrowing down our actual locations, of course we had to change the way we had visualized many of the shots.

RP: When you evaluated a location, what factors would you consider?

AS: First and foremost, I would try to determine whether the space could accommodate everything we wanted to do. For instance, we considered filming the scenes in Lulu's slum apartment in the same location we were using for Izzy's apartment. But when I sat down and really thought about the visual elements of the shot, I realized we needed a space that was much wider so that the camera would be able to move about and accommodate the actors as they walked around. If we were to adapt the scene to this location, we would have to make some significant visual sacrifices. So we began our search for Lulu's apartment all over again—until we found the location on East Sixth Street, which worked practically with our theoretical designs.

RP: Talking about theory and practice, what about the special effects scenes?

AS: What was most difficult about these scenes was that we needed to visualize something that didn't exist outside of Paul's imagination. Somehow we had to arrive at a sort of group consensus about the stone's appearance so that we could set about creating its image on screen. While the digital-effects company was responsible for altering the image of the actual stone, we needed to colorize the surrounding environment through gels. The problem with gels, and particularly with deep blue gels, is that they severely amend the normal curve of so-called white light. Thus, when the white light, by way of gelling, was turned into a strong blue light, it affected the emulsion layer of the film, resulting in the loss of sharpness. The gels also absorb such intense amounts of heat from the lights during the course of a shot that the blue hue begins to bleach out and the gels change color while the camera is rolling. If we had had all the money in the world, I would have chosen to photograph the scenes without such effects and colorize them digitally in a virtual environment. That way, you retain definition and have more control over the image in general.

RP: You referred earlier to *Lulu*'s complex infrastructure. From a visual perspective, how did you try to untangle the film's various layers?

172

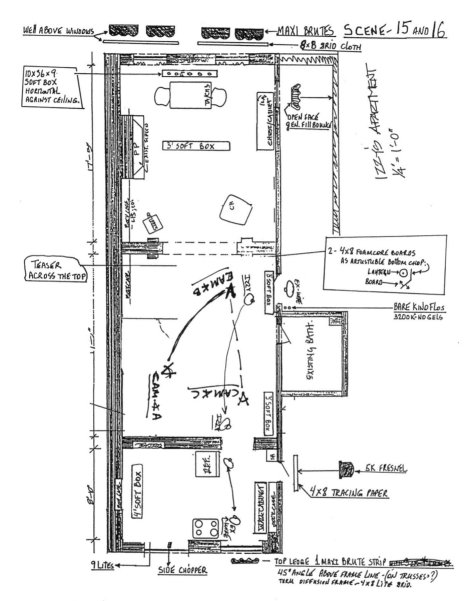

WELL ABOVE WINDOWS →

MAXI BRUTES — SCENE-15 AND 16

MAXI BRUTES

← 8×8 GRID CLOTH

10×36×9
SOFT BOX
HORIZONTAL
AGAINST CEILING.

IZZIE'S APARTMENT
¼" = 1'-0"

TAKE-TH

3' SOFT BOX

CHEST/CABINET

OPEN FACE
GEN. FILL BOUNCE

EXIST. SPICES

P.P.

17'-2"

BACKLINE — LED.50W

CH

2 - 4×8 FOAMCORE BOARDS
AS ADJUSTABLE BOTTOM CHOP:
LANTERN
BOARD

TEASER
ACROSS THE TOP

CAM+B

3' SOFT BOX

30W

BARE KINO FLOS
3200 K- NO GELS

12'-0"

5×5 BATH

CAM-+ A

CAM+C

3' SOFT BOX

5A

8'-0"

4' SOFT BOX

5K FRESNEL

4×8 TRACING PAPER

9 LITES →

SIDE CHOPPER

TOP LEDGE 1 MAXI BRUTE STRIP
45° ANGLE ABOVE FRAME LINE - (ON TRUSSES?)
THRU DIFFUSION FRAME - 4×8 LITE GRID.

REVISED

AS: It was very important to me to make Celia's world and Izzy's world clearly distinct. Otherwise, we would deprive the film of its visual resonance. Izzy's world is very complex. His character is going through many stages of development; he is in a constant state of tug-of-war with himself. He carries so much baggage with him that his world is heavy, and I hope this is reflected visually in his apartment. I think it was an important decision to photograph it the way we did.

RP: Which was to underlight it?

AS: There are two ways of showing emotion: explicitly or suggestively. If I lit Izzy in such a way that every single nuance of emotion was revealed, the viewer might very quickly lose interest. Suggestive reality can be much more powerful. Harvey is such a fine physical actor that I quickly realized I could just create the suggestion of his world through underlighting and leave the rest to the audience. For example, if I had used a front light to photograph the scene where Izzy is sitting in his apartment when the telephone rings, it would not have drawn you in to the same degree.

RP: As you shot it, it's a closer reflection of his state of emotional withdrawal.

AS: Exactly. I hate to make these sorts of comparisons, but Rembrandt also underlit many of his portraits in such a way that you become intrigued and want to study the figure very closely and intently. This is the effect I wanted to create with Izzy. For instance, the scene where Izzy discovers the dead body is also very, very dark. In the end, his reaction reveals what's happened, but the actual passage of Izzy going to the body is more like an etching, a suggestion. You can imagine this scene as a vacuum in time and space, deprived of all sounds but a selective few: footsteps, a passing car in the distance, a dog barking or somebody screaming. It is this minimalism that gives the scene its emotional power. If you were to show every single detail on the screen, it would be boring.

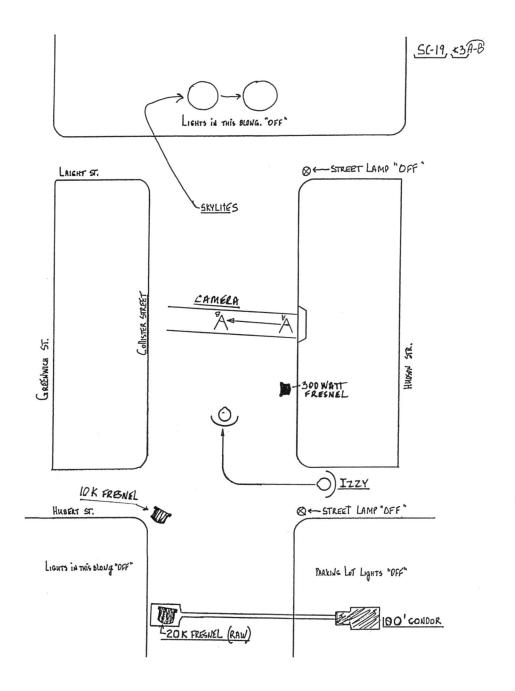

SC-19, ⟨3 A-B⟩

LIGHTS IN THIS BLDNG. "OFF"

LAIGHT ST.

STREET LAMP "OFF"

SKYLITES

CAMERA

COLLISTER STREET

GREENWICH ST.

HUDSON STR.

300 WATT FRESNEL

IZZY

10 K FRESNEL

HUBERT ST.

STREET LAMP "OFF"

LIGHTS IN THIS BLDNG "OFF"

PARKING LOT LIGHTS "OFF"

20 K FRESNEL (RAW)

100' CONDOR

RP: What about Celia's world?

AS: I didn't mind showing Celia's environment as much as we did because Celia is a person who is comfortable in her world, who is comfortable with herself. Celia is just comfortable. There is a simplicity and a goodness to her, and I wanted to reflect this in her environment. I tried to make the world around her appear very soft and natural, as if the camera were just there to record the facts. I wanted the naturalism of Celia's environment to be in utter contrast to the world in which she finds herself as Lulu. Through lighting, I really tried to distinguish Lulu's universe from the reality of the rest of the film.

RP: The film was shot with a lot of coverage for each scene. Was this a decision you and Paul came to together?

AS: It was mainly Paul's decision. I think he wanted to prevent getting stuck in a situation where he had no choices in the editing room. Now, seeing the film and the way it's been constructed, I realize what an important decision this was. I tend to adhere to the school of minimal coverage, but this leaves the director and editor with almost no choices. Unless the script is written with such precision that you know exactly what you are going to use every single word for, you'd be shooting yourself in the foot not to give yourself options. Nonetheless, there are moments in the film where we decided that coverage was not really that important and we shot the scene in one. I think there is actually a very beautiful cohesion to these shots. Because, if you consider certain scenes in the film, for instance when Celia finds out she got the part of Lulu, they can't be dissected—they have to play out in one. These little moments in the film are very descriptive, and they pull you along with their visual continuity.

RP: Would you consider the last scene of the film one of these moments?

AS: Definitely. In this scene, I really wanted to connect Celia and the ambulance. I filmed Celia's walk with a steadicam so that the moment the ambulance went by, the camera was able to swoop right around Celia and end up on the back of the ambulance as it drives away from us. I think the shot creates the sense of a circular connection between them that I find very beautiful and very cohesive to the work.

RP: I love the fluid opening of scene 23, where Izzy and Celia are in bed together for the first time. The scene begins with a tight shot of a photograph of Celia and then sweeps out around the room to bring the viewer to the characters in a very intimate, involving manner.

AS: Paul never wanted to cut into the scene abruptly. He wanted the camera to uncover something about Celia that we didn't know; by holding on a picture of Celia in a tutu, it tells us something about who Celia is. I thought it was a wonderful idea. A person's environment reveals so much about a person. It's like, "Show me your apartment, and I'll tell you who you are." So that was Paul's idea. It was not a very complex setup, but I find it very elegant and eloquent.

RP: Paul said that when he first mentioned his idea for the "black limbo" hospital bed in scene 4 that your eyes "lit up." How did you go about implementing this idea?

AS: Since we did not have the option of using special effects for this scene, we had to find a way to create something physically by virtue of the optics. With a 17-mm lens on the camera, a lot of extraneous elements entered the frame: stands, the grid, the entire width and height of the stage, and everything else that was around. It was not until the actual day of the shoot that I realized there was a way of photographing the scene using a zoom lens and a fixed hard matte. We used a wide-angle end of a zoom lens and blocked all extraneous elements like the ceiling, the floor, and the lights with a hard matte constructed from black flags. Essentially, we created a rectangular window in the center of these flags. By deepening the t-stop, I was able to match the black level of the background to the black level of the foreground's hard matte. I gave precise instructions to the laboratory to print it "down"; thus the foreground matte seamlessly blended into the background limbo. The end result was that we did not see the actual window created with the black flags. If the stage had afforded us the possibility of photographing the scene with a wide-angle lens in complete limbo, then I would have just dollied in, as opposed to using the zoom. But considering that we were so limited in our options, the zoom actually solved a big problem for us. It produced basically the same effect.

RP: What were the techniques you used in scene 10 to convey a sense of Izzy's disorientation?

AS: The problem this scene posed was how to photograph Izzy's shoes from his point of view without Harvey having to carry the camera. The only plausible way of doing it was to have Lukasz Jogalla, the camera operator, impersonate Harvey. It turned out that they wore the same shoe size, so we got Lukasz into Izzy's Hush Puppies and enrolled him in the Harvey Keitel School of Walking. I think Lukasz did a great job. When you see the scene on the big screen, you certainly don't suspect that it's not Harvey walking there.

RP: There are quite a few scenes in the film in which Izzy is shot from above, for instance in the hospital and in his apartment. What did you wish to suggest through this shot?

AS: The bird's-eye view is very important, since it objectifies the image. In the hospital scene, we cut from the subjective point of view of Izzy to the aerial shot and then back to the subjective. Cutting away to the objective shot like this calls attention to the fact that you are within somebody's world; you start to see that world a little differently and to understand its boundaries. It is a way of making the viewer step back from the film, of putting him in an "angelic" position, so to speak.

RP: Paul often talks about this "crazy story" that he's written. How do you interpret it?

AS: I think the story is primarily about loss, but it is also a story that asks: "If I could live my life again, how would I live it?" Izzy is at the threshold of death and he is reliving his life the way he wishes it had been. So, if it is a dream, it is a dream of the events that he never experienced but always wanted to. You always ask yourself the question, "If I had another chance at life, what would I do differently?" In a nutshell, that is what the story is about.

RP: What were the greatest influences on your development as a cinematographer?

AS: Russian cinema, without a doubt. Not because I come from Russia but because cinema in Russia was treated as an art form. Even within the confines of propaganda, there was a handful of artists who managed to express visions of the most incredible human depth. For instance, there is a film called *Shadows of Our Forgotten Ancestors* by Sergei Paradzhanov, which is really a very simple love story set in the Carpathian Mountains. Yet this simplicity belies the complexity of its structure. The film is incredibly layered, both visually and textually, but is constructed with such subtlety that these layers do not call attention to themselves. It is through this subtlety that you begin to understand how the film works, and once you do, you can't help but be transformed by it. The same goes for Tarkovsky, who I really do think was a genius. People accuse him of symbolism, but when you truly begin to understand his films, you realize there were no symbols there; he was simply creating his own unique world that reflected his personal convictions.

To bring this back to Paul's work, Paul has a voice. Nobody else writes like Paul—or Paul doesn't write like anybody else—this is what is invigorating about his work. I can say the same thing about all the filmmakers who've touched me; they all have their own language and their own signature. The reason why I absolutely love Tarkovsky, Abuladze, Paradjanov, Antonioni, Bergman, and Bresson, just to name a few, is because their films express this sort of personal, poetic judgment. And this is what really involves me in cinema, the signature of an auteur. Because cinema is not a conveyor process. To me, the whole problem with Hollywood is that there is no signature after the end of the film. It is an assembly line where films are just being made according to the formula, and the more formulaic the film, the more money it is going to make.

RP: Did you study cinematography in Russia or America?

AS: When I was twelve, my parents gave me a still camera and signed me up to study photography in the after-school program. I went to these classes on and off for four years and learned the basics of photographic sensitometry, exposure techniques, black-and-white processing and printing. After high school, I was studying philology and philosophy at university when, for personal reasons, I decided to volunteer for military service in the Soviet army. I was recruited into the photography unit and received film training there.

RP: So how did you begin your career when you came to America?

AS: My first job in America was pumping gas. When I first came, I didn't speak the language, so the most important thing was to study English. I worked in pizza parlors, McDonald's, all sorts of little jobs. I worked for three years at the Crawford Watch Company on Canal Street fixing watches and clocks, during which time I was able to save some money. With my savings I bought an Ikegami professional video camera and, subsequently, an Eclair 16-mm.-film camera. In 1984–1985, using ¾" video equipment, I made a documentary on Russian immigrants in Brighton Beach called *The Russian Touch*. Manhattan Cable broadcast it, which was a great achievement for me. Not that I made any money from it, but it gave me a little exposure— a few people watched it! With this credit, I was hired by JC Penney Communications as a camera operator/lighting designer and was paid $175 a day. I felt that I had attained the highest reaches of the United States—considering that I had been working six or seven days a week at Crawford making $200 per week. It was only a monetary success, that's all, but it meant a lot to me then. Among the many corporate clients of JC Penney Communications were Nabisco and IBM. I got in touch with their in-house production departments and was soon working as a lighting-cameraman on videos that were used to introduce their new products at corporate events. Through this connection, I came in contact with a lot of independent producers. Naturally, I wanted to be back doing narrative work in film. I did some smaller-budget music videos and commercials and was able to build up my commercial reel. Then, in 1990–1991, I got my first job as director of photography on John Raffo's *Big and Mean,* and it's all gone from there.

RP: To what degree do you feel your Russian background has shaped your cinematic aesthetic?

AS: Growing up in Moscow, the only Western films the government allowed us to see were those depicting the ills of capitalist society, so my main exposure was to films produced domestically. No matter how appallingly patriotic many of them might have been, these films were at least complex to the degree that your mind had to become involved in order to resolve everything that was going on. But I think architecture and literature had a much greater influence on my aesthetic than cinema. Russia is steeped in this phenomenal history. In Moscow we were surrounded by the grandeur of Byzantium architecture, which I view as very organic. There is a softness to its "style" and "form," so to speak. When you walk around Moscow in the fall and you see these buildings in the rolling fog and gray light, your thinking develops in a certain way. Aesthetically, I respond to this dreamy, hypnotic world that I was exposed to as a child; these are the images that formed me.

Four years ago we went to Russia. We were in the middle of nowhere, four hundred miles north of Moscow, in a little village where my brother has a tiny *izba* hut. To enter this village, you have to cover about twelve kilometers on foot through a very wooded area. My wife and I had walked about seven or eight kilometers when suddenly this glorious, majestic, maternal landscape opened up to our view. We came out of the forest and looked at this breathtaking still-life expanse of the river running away from us toward the horizon, at the beautiful, tall grass that was swaying very gently in the wind, at the gray, leaden sky hanging above us. You look at that stuff and you are transfixed; you are in another world. It is so hypnotic. Your knees cave in and you just have to sit down and absorb it all. You feel so at peace with yourself. I don't know what it is. It's like being in the womb. It was the quietest and most fulfilling moment of my life. When I think about images, I think about images like that.

January 14, 1998

Kalina Ivanov
production designer

Rebecca Prime: You'd worked with Paul before as the production designer on *Smoke* and *Blue in the Face*. How did your involvement with *Lulu on the Bridge* begin?

Kalina Ivanov: It all started with a phone call from Paul. I was working in South Carolina last summer when he called me up and said: "I have a project for you. Could you read it over the weekend?" We were on location and shooting six days a week, so I told him that it might take me a little while to get to it. But Paul was adamant that I read the script immediately, and so I did, of course, as Paul is a dear friend. I was so intrigued by the script that I delayed my dinner plans that night in order to finish reading it. That's the best sign about a script.

RP: Were you responding to the possibilities the script offered from a design perspective?

KI: When selecting my projects, I try to seek out well-written, character-driven scripts with intellectual and emotional depth, and *Lulu* is certainly all this. But yes, the more times you read the script, the more you understand that it is an absolute designers' piece. It runs the range of every imaginable set you can think of, from rich to poor, theatrical to realistic. We had to find a style that seemed natural and yet somehow also conveyed that there was something happening on a second level, that you weren't exactly watching a slice of life. We could have chosen to give it a surrealistic feel, but Paul made it clear to me that he wanted the film to be grounded in reality. He didn't want to reveal the magical element to the audience right away—but rather to allow it to slowly build in their hearts.

You see this approach in much of Paul's writing, I think. He has a remarkable sense of how bizarre, chance events can transform and shape the lives of the most real, human characters. He's not a surrealist, yet there is certainly a magical quality about his writing. And as an artist, if I didn't believe in magic, I wouldn't be doing what I do!

RP: Perhaps because Paul's also a novelist, the script includes more detailed descriptions than usual. Did you find this a help or a hindrance?

KI: It actually made my job easier, since I didn't always have to try to guess what he had in mind. Paul is a great communicator. Although he had very specific ideas about how he saw these sets, right down to what some of the colors should be, he never confined my vision. We had a few disagreements, but that's all part of the creative process. If we didn't have any, then I would say there was something wrong with the two of us!

RP: What aspects of the film did you find most challenging?

KI: The many layers of reality in the film posed very interesting and provocative questions for me as an artist. I needed to find a way to resolve these realities without telegraphing their ultimate resolution. Yet in order for this resolution to seem organic and natural, it had to be incorporated somehow throughout the body of the film. Otherwise, the audience would feel that we'd pulled the rug out from under them.

RP: So you had to find a way to integrate and interrelate these alternate realities. Where did you begin?

KI: I started looking around for inspiration, and for some reason the painter that I really connected to was Francis Bacon. It's inevitable that when I read a script, an image forms in my mind; a color, a painter, a mood comes to me. I thought that Francis Bacon was a good reference for this movie because, on the one hand, he is a portraitist, which is a traditional, formal discipline, while, on the other hand, his work is extremely experimental and emotional. Izzy Maurer seemed to me like a Francis Bacon character; he lived in that sort of dark, oppressive world, and he desperately needed to be rescued from it. This woman who comes into his life is a ray of hope, a true breath of fresh air. She is what saves him from the deep depression he has fallen into. And although Bacon uses a very dark palette, his paintings always have a line of brightness running through them as a contrast. So I started working from this painter. I wanted to try to bring those same combinations of simplicity and formality, of expressionism and emotion to the set.

RP: What was your next step after Francis Bacon?

KI: The first thing I needed to resolve was how to begin creating the palette. Because the magical stone acts as the catalyst for the narrative, I thought it should provide the film's dominant, conceptual color. Once Paul and I had agreed on what that color was, it very much determined the look for the rest of the film. We chose a very particular blue, and I knew I could explore the cooler tones without being cold. For instance, the purple curtains in the night club are a variation on that blue. I really tried to subtly incorporate the color throughout the movie, to use it as a reference point so that the film as a whole would support the concept of the stone.

Then there is this issue of the film within the film, the new version of *Pandora's Box*. The original is such a landmark film that attempting to remake it would be like trying to redo *Metropolis*. There are a few movies in film history that are absolutely seminal to every filmmaker and *Pandora's Box* is one of them. So I didn't want to get to know the original too well. I just watched it once and then put it away. What I decided to capture from Pabst's film was the sense of grandeur. In the story, what is important is the fact that Lulu starts in a very high place and descends to a very low place. So I decided to use the large proportions of art deco to evoke the expressionistic style of the era but at the same time to make the set contemporary, something you might also see today.

RP: In order to develop a cohesive palette for the film, you must have collaborated very closely with Adelle (Bonny) Lutz, the costume designer, and Alik Sakharov, the director of photography. . . .

K I: One of the most pleasurable things about this project was the fact that all three of us constantly talked to each other and developed our palettes together. Each set, be it a location or a construction, had its own palette and had to refer visually back to the stone. Once I had determined a palette for the sets, I made a copy and gave it to Bonny so that she could work off of it. If you look carefully in the movie, you will see that we never clashed and that, as a matter of fact, Bonny's costumes had the same character as the sets. It is to Bonny's credit that she is the sort of artist who is able to collaborate so closely with other artists. Alik and I were also able to help each other a great deal. By planning our work together in advance, I was able to incorporate lighting into my sets, which saves a lot of time later on.

R P: The French production designer Eugene Lourie described scenic design as the art "not of making pictures but of relating them to living presences." Would you agree?

K I: Completely. The way I work is as a detective. In my mind, I follow the characters around and delve into their back stories. I want to know everything about a character. If the director doesn't have the answers or doesn't have the time to give me the answers, then I will invent my own past for the character. I also like to talk with the actors, if they are willing, because they tend to use a similar approach toward their own work. I try to put all the little pieces of information together in order to form a total picture of the character, and then I provide these clues in my set. They are subliminally there, even if the audience doesn't notice them. Even if they never end up on screen, as often happens, their presence is still important, because it gives a reality to the actor. These details define the character for them, and they define the character for us.

The different levels of reality in the film are all determined by the characters. Izzy's world is absolutely based around Izzy's character. Who is this man? He is a lone wolf, he is a dead soul. He doesn't connect with people, he's not even interested in his music anymore. So for his place, we wanted to capture the anonymous feeling of a hotel room. We didn't even give him cabinets for his clothes—just put some hooks on the wall from which he could hang his stuff. There were also some very surreal accents, such as the big photograph of Ireland on the wall. It doesn't say Ireland on it, but subliminally it's important. So although it was a very realistic set, there were certain subtle touches that you can't possibly understand until you get to the end of the movie.

Then there's Celia's reality. Celia is the future; she is the one who walks away at the end of the film. Therefore, we wanted her apartment to have a sense of simplicity and hope, to be an environment that felt comfortable. Since she's young and doesn't have much money, we bought most of her furniture at IKEA—a lot of people will probably recognize her coffee table! But the colors were lavender and pale yellow, which are not exactly the colors everyone uses to paint their apartment. As in Izzy's apartment, we included some symbolic touches. For instance, Paul brought in a poster of a Renaissance painting depicting Adam and Eve being thrown out of the Garden of Eden. You wouldn't notice the symbolism while watching the movie the first time, but you will definitely see it on a second viewing.

Concerning the film within the film, it was important to determine who decided that look. Since Vanessa Redgrave played the director, I saw the film as a woman's version of *Pandora's Box,* which inspired me to use a very warm and inviting palette. With the exception of the photo loft, the other sets all use lots of wood and warm browns and oranges. I didn't think that a woman directing *Pandora's Box* would be likely to give it a cold, glossy, Hollywood look. Women's films in general tend to be more personal, so I tried to give this *Pandora's Box* a more intimate feel and yet evoke the grand proportions of the Pabst original.

RP: The photo loft is one of the most visually stunning sets in the film, sort of *Blow-Up* meets *2001.* What was the concept behind this design?

KI: It all started with Paul. He and Alik came up to me and said that they wanted an extremely bright, vibrantly white void. But I felt that a plain white space would have a danger of looking too symbolic; I didn't want it to seem like heaven. So instead I designed a very the-atrical, three-walled set. What is unusual about the set is that it is asymmetrical; the wall on one side is higher than the wall on the other side. It's always a good idea to make a model to see how a set works three-dimensionally. As we developed the model for this set, it was clear that it needed something like a vertical line to divide the space. So we added this very beautiful column, a simple architectural element that split the set in two uneven parts and helped root it, if not in reality, at least not in heaven!

RP: Do you have a favorite set?

KI: Probably the most sophisticated, meaningful sets were the simplest ones, because they were driven by the psychology of the characters. Form without content is ultimately shallow, and I would like to think that my work tries to reach for a deeper understanding of character and story and of film as a language. But on a purely visual level, I did enjoy the film within the film. I loved Shine and Lulu's bedroom just because no one ever lives in those kinds of bedrooms. Only movie characters. No one sleeps in a forty-by-forty-foot room, at least not in Manhattan! I also loved the minimalism of the photo loft. I love sim-plicity, I really do. If I could do a set with just one chair, I would be so happy. But it would have to be the absolutely perfect chair for the character!

RP: Here's the question I've been asking everyone: how do you inter-pret the story?

KI: I think the story is fundamentally very hopeful. It is a story of redemption. We have a character who has lost himself, who has for-gotten he was a human being. He learns that the most important thing is to live through your heart, and he's able to find happiness at the last moment. Yes, there are all these crazy levels that can take you in a thousand different directions, but the basic heart of it is quite simple. I think these sorts of films are harder to finance because people don't like to be surprised and shown unexpected things. But ultimately, these are the movies we remember. These are our favorite movies.

CUT TO:

(24/5) MS - CELIA
SHE REACHES TOWARD
THE STONE, BUT DOESN'T
TOUCH IT YET.
(digital effect)
C: "BE quiet"...
I: "Don't touch it"...

24/5

CUT TO:

(24/6) MS (LOWER ANGLE) - CELIA
SHE SITS DOWN ON THE
COUCH AND SLIDES HER
PALM UNDER THE STONE
C: "...How could I not touch it?"
(digital effect)

24/6

INTERCUT WITH:

24/7 LS - IZZY (in silhouette)
He's watching her
J: "What does it feel like?"
(blue light SFX)

24/7

CUT TO:

24/8 MCU - CELIA (slight high angle)
SHE'S laughing softly
(stone is out of frame)
C: "Oh, come on. Don't be
afraid."

24/8

Ⓒ

RP: Growing up in Bulgaria, what sort of films were you exposed to?

KI: For many years, the only foreign films allowed in Bulgaria were classic films from the twenties, thirties, and forties, primarily French movies and the Marx Brothers. They were screened without subtitles, but there was always a translator, usually a rather old woman. The Marx Brothers would be difficult to translate into any language because they use so much wordplay, but then imagine this poor old woman struggling to keep up with the dialogue! It was all very comical and surreal, which basically describes what it was like growing up in Bulgaria. It was definitely a surreal environment. Right before I left in the mid-seventies, there was a period when Communism began to thaw of its own accord and more foreign films started to be shown. The movies that really impressed me as a teenager were *The Conversation* by Francis Ford Coppola, *Last Year at Marienbad* by Alain Resnais, and Antonioni's *The Passenger*. A strange combination, but these films made me realize for the first time just how powerful and meaningful cinema can be. I wouldn't say these films necessarily inspired me to become a designer, but they gave me my first awareness of the importance of the images and of the symbiosis between camera and design.

RP: How would you say your background has influenced your cinematic sensibilities?

KI: I would say that my Bulgarian childhood always shows up in my palette. I love color, and I often look at Bulgarian icons and kilims for inspiration. For example, in *Lulu* I chose a lot of ethnic rugs and red-orange tones for Philip Kleinman's loft. It gave the character warmth and showed that he had traveled all over the world. . . . In general, I tend to select projects that stimulate me intellectually; I never worry if they are going to be commercially successful. One thing I know is that human beings are full of contradictions—this is the most interesting thing about them. I think this is something Paul captures really well, this sort of three-dimensional thinking.

January 27, 1998

Adelle Lutz
costume designer

Rebecca Prime: When you first read a script, do you have a strong sartorial sense of the characters?

Adelle Lutz: Not at all! The first time I read a script, I have absolutely no clue what anyone is wearing. So I ask a lot of questions. Knowing what's important to the director and the production designer gives me a starting point to work from. On a job interview, if I'm asked how I see a certain character dressed, I'm tempted to respond: "Beats me! Why don't you tell me?" I have to do much more preparation before I can answer a question like that. I read and reread the script, I go to the library. For this film, I looked at as many jazz books as I could find and read up on the original *Lulu* plays. It is really a matter of doing your research.

I also try to break down each character the way an actor might—that Stella Adler training in script analysis is hard to shake! How does the character feel about religion, about families? If this person were voting, would he vote Republican or Democrat? Would he even vote? Does he spend all his money on drugs or shoes? We all have these quirks, and I try to figure out what they are for each particular character.

RP: Do you confer with the actors during this process?

AL: Of course. They have to be comfortable in the skin that I'm giving them.

RP: Does this mean they just have to like the jacket you've picked out for them or do they also have to share your understanding of the character wearing the jacket?

AL: Both. With *Lulu*, I'd been mulling over the characters and the themes for weeks when, suddenly, fireworks started popping in my head and all the pieces clicked into place. This was really thrilling and exciting for me, and I think my enthusiasm rolled over to Paul. He encouraged me to speak to the actors about how I saw their characters conceptually and symbolically, and about why I thought particular looks could work in this film.

RP: Can you describe this epiphany?

AL: When I detached the characters from their everyday reality and looked at them in a larger context, I realized that Izzy represents the past. Even before he's shot, his life is over in the sense that he has nothing to look forward to. Therefore, the look that I developed for him is a past-tense look. He is most comfortable in clothes from his past—khakis, old shirts. His colors are those of the tobacco he smokes, of the bourbon he drinks. Celia represents the future and all the possibilities of life and love, so I thought her look should be clean and modern. But I also wanted to indicate that there was something a bit different about her, something more exotic, and so I designed that little brocade Mandarin jacket—in blue. Because of Celia's relation to the stone, I decided to base her palette around the cooler tones. Lulu is the absolute present—the pure, animal reaction. I tried to incorporate a different part of the animal kingdom into each of her costumes. We see her in a leopard fur–lined evening gown, in a flesh-colored cobra-print sarong, in a wedding dress with peacock feathers. And for her death scene, I trimmed her sweater with human hair cut from a wig. I thought it would be appropriate for her to die as a human being. She lives as an animal, but dies as a person.

RP: How did you determine the palettes for the other characters?

AL: The other characters grew from Izzy and Celia. For instance, I based Hannah's palette around burgundies and maroons as a way of linking her to the tobacco-stained world of Izzy's past. It also emphasized the opposition with the blues tones of Celia's world. In building up the characters, it's up to me to put together their history. Because Izzy is played by Harvey Keitel and Hannah by Gina Gershon, there is clearly an age difference between these characters. How long ago were they married? How long were they married for? These are the sorts of questions I try to answer. I was actually quite stumped by Hannah—I couldn't manage to find her in my costume mind's-eye. Luckily for me, my husband is a musician. When I presented him with my problem, his immediate response was, "Well, she's got to be a Village bohemian." The minute he said that, I understood who Hannah was, why she was attracted to Izzy, and why it didn't work. I knew what her colors would be, what kind of jewelry she would wear. She probably had tattoos on her butt—definitely a very different sort of woman than Celia!

Once I had figured out Hannah, I had to consider Philip Kleinman. Obviously, Hannah has grown up since she was with Izzy. Now she's with this savvy film producer, and I needed to figure out what the glue was that held them together. I decided that it was an interest in the exotic. When I suggested this to Kalina, she helped consolidate the idea by prominently featuring those Indian photographs in her set for Kleinman's apartment. When Izzy asks Hannah where she got her tan, I imagine that she and Philip just got back from a trip to some remote place, like Brazil. I had some Bahian amulet ribbons that I picked up in Brazil a few years ago, so I tied these around their wrists. Nobody in the audience will ever notice, but it is very satisfying to me to know they are there.

RP: Someone asked me about the skullcap worn by Dave Reilly (Richard Edson), the drummer in Izzy's band, who I also noticed wears a blue Egyptian ankh around his neck. Any symbolism here?

AL: Because of Izzy's "situation," I thought it would be fun and interesting to use some religious symbols, whether they be Tibetan, Indian, or Turkish, to suggest the reality of Izzy's dream. Little things here and there that maybe nobody else will notice, but that all add up. As with the wall of photos in the bathroom, I wanted Izzy to be surrounded on stage by everything that he sees after he is shot. Another one of the musicians wears a snakeskin shirt that Izzy could then transform into Lulu's serpentine sarong. I wanted all the "dream" references to be present in reality.

RP: Did you ever visualize a costume or a scene completely differently from what Paul had in mind?

AL: One moment when I disagreed with Paul was the final scene of the film, where Celia watches the ambulance go by. I wanted Celia to be dramatically different from the Celia we'd seen before, to have absolutely nothing to do with the Celia we knew. But Paul thought it was important that there be a sense of connection and continuity. I have no complaints about the way it is—it's interesting how the story invites so many different readings. I wanted to put some major sappy melodrama into the movie, but fortunately, Paul's a bit cleaner than I am.

RP: What was the greatest challenge for you on this film?

AL: The film within the film. To give these sections a different textural feel, Paul and Alik planned to use certain colored gels. A week or so before production, we scheduled a test day so that we could see how the colors and materials we were thinking of using in these scenes read on film with the gels. And it was a good thing we did! For instance, in the bedroom scene, I had selected a bright, fire-engine red for Lulu's gown. We all thought it was perfect, but when we tested the fabric, it came up black—absolutely all the light had been sucked out of it. So I began to look for more light-reflective fabrics and found this wonderful red-gold cloth at an ecclesiastical store called La Lamé. My husband couldn't believe it that every priest in the U.S. has to buy his fabric from a shop called La Lamé!

RP: Do you prefer to buy your costumes or create your own designs?

AL: I like to build my costumes—often, it's easier to make what you want than to buy it. In a town like New York where half the people only wear black, you can imagine the trouble I had finding a blue skirt for Celia in the middle of winter! Another factor you have to consider is the need for multiples of certain items. For instance, take Izzy's shirt in the jazz club. We bought a bunch of white shirts and dyed them exactly the same shade of yellow. Because Izzy is shot in the scene and the shirt becomes stained, we needed to be sure we had a clean shirt prepared for each take. We also had to set aside a number of shirts for the props department to rig with blood—underneath his breast pocket they put squibs that explode the moment he is shot. Then there is the shirt for the close-up of Izzy lying on the floor after he is shot, the shirt for when he is being carried to the ambulance, and so on. We needed to have all these different shirts to accurately reflect the spread of blood from the wound.

Because the film is not shot sequentially, we rely on the wardrobe department to ensure continuity for scenes like these. I just design the costumes—they are responsible for maintaining the look of the film. They have all these tools from cat-hair brushes to little picks to hair spray. They distress all the clothing so that even the shoes of a minor character look worn. It's almost a kind of art form—they are real alchemists.

RP: Do you have a favorite costume?

AL: I'd have to say the peacock dress. It's my favorite because it was the hardest to figure out. When I started designing the wedding dress, I included a feather headdress, something out of *Swan Lake*. The feather idea expanded into a bodice, then a skirt, until finally I remembered these albino peacocks I'd once seen in Mexico, and I knew what the feathers had to be. As albino peacock feathers are not available in mass quantities; I arranged to have some normal peacock feathers bleached—after first making sure that they didn't have to kill the peacocks! While the feathers came out a nice shade of ivory, the eyes had bleached to gold, which made them unreadable from a distance. So my assistants and I spent hours hand-painting the eyes various shades of blue.

I knew I wanted to feathers to spill out like a fan from the back of

Lulu Weds

THINNER
SILK
SELF
PIPE

DOUBLE LAYER

4 PLY
SILK
CREPE IN CREAM

TRAIL →
FLOOR

BLEACHED &
REPAINTED
PEACOCK FEATHER
TRAIN
MUST BE
COLLAPSABLE.
FAN

·ON GOLD/SILVER
THREADED
NETTING
TO KEEP
WEIGHTLESS
CLIP FEATHERS →
8-10"

HAS TO
'SWISH'

the dress, but I didn't have a clue how to do it. So I took the material and the feathers to John Schneeman, whom I'd worked with before, and told him what I needed. It was a real feat of engineering. For instance, if he used the full length of the feathers, the weight would drag on Mira's back. So we cut the feathers to about eight inches. John figured it all out—what sort of cut we needed, how to do it without wires. The dress turned out to be something we were all equally proud of. We invested so much work in it—painting each frigging feather by hand! You only see it on screen for a few seconds, but if it weren't there, it would make a big difference.

RP: What do you aspire to in your work?

AL: Just to remain true to the vision of the material and the director. If I can bring the characters to life in a way that supports the director's vision, then I'm satisfied. I want to be true to the story that we're trying to tell. I love independent filmmaking because there is less risk that the director's vision will become corrupted or diluted than there is with a studio production. When you have too much money, you also have too many opinions!

RP: When you're dragging yourself to the set at 5:00 A.M. on a Monday morning, how do you justify your career choice to yourself?

AL: It gives me my dose of circus life! To use another comparison, I think of it like going into battle. You line up behind the general, look to the right, look to the left, and then you're off. You can't stop until you get to the end, even though sometimes you know that you're fighting the wrong battle and that you're not going to emerge unsullied. But there is something about the camaraderie and the collaborative spirit that is unique to film and very wonderful. You're living on adrenaline and lack of sleep, on glowing orange foods. That's why I like working in film—because of the glowing orange food!

February 17, 1998

Tim Squyres
editor

Rebecca Prime: "Films are made in the editing room"—true or false?

Tim Squyres: There are enormous limits to what an editor can do. Certainly, you can do a lot to help performances and smooth transitions, even to alter the artistic tone of a film. But at the end of the day, you can only work with what comes in the door.

RP: Sort of like editing a book . . . except that, of course, the material you receive is the result of a collaborative effort. When deciding whether or not to take on a project, is there one factor in this collaboration that you weigh more heavily than the others?

TS: Definitely the script. I need to find it compelling enough to spend the next five or six months working on it. Unlike other jobs in the movies, it's not possible as an editor to divorce yourself from the project as a whole and just focus on your aspect of it. For instance, a film can have a lousy script but nonetheless present very interesting and challenging work for a set designer. But editing comprises every aspect of the film—its emotions become part of your daily experience. I know a woman who was working on a documentary about spousal abuse for a year and a half, and it changed her whole life. Eventually, she just had to stop. So it's important not only to see the value of the material, but to be happy to live with it. Otherwise, you'd have to give yourself a major pep talk just to get out of bed each morning.

RP: So with *Lulu* you didn't think you'd need the pep talk?

TS: The films I had most recently worked on had been very realistic in style and emotional in content, and *Lulu* looked like it was going to offer the opportunity to do something different. There is an important intellectual component to this film that I found very engaging. I liked the themes about right and wrong, about taking responsibility for your life—"Am I a good person or a bad person?" Those kinds of questions are exactly what the film is about, and I found that very interesting, very compelling. Another important reason I took the film was because I felt that Paul and I could really work well together.

RP: I know Paul and Alik were quite assiduous in their preparations, mapping out the whole film in shot lists, and so on. Were you involved in this process?

TS: I tried to know exactly what they had in mind and to anticipate any problems that might arise. Although it's very hard to tell what a scene will actually look like from a shot list, I was concerned with some of the longer camera moves they had planned. These moves can be very lovely and stately, but unless they move the story forward, eventually they'll be dropped. Because sooner or later, anything that doesn't directly affect the story is a candidate for cutting—even if it's good. Setting up these moves can take half the shooting day, leaving you scrambling to get the rest of the scene. And most likely, the part that you scramble for is all you'll end up using. So a little foresight can be helpful.

RP: What is your role during production?

TS: On this film, I would attend dailies and note Paul's comments on each take. Although we often wound up not using the takes that we had thought were best during the dailies, it's good to have these notes as a reference. But we would rarely talk about a scene's structure, and, even if we had, I would have ignored it. I wouldn't have been doing my job otherwise, because it is important for me to try and give everything a shot. Mostly we discussed the rough edits I'd given Paul the day before. I would much rather talk about the material after I've had a go at it.

RP: When making the rough edits, would it be with a preconceived idea of the scene in mind?

TS: I'll have an idea in my head of how I want to structure the scene, but I try not to think about it—you don't want to prevent yourself from seeing other possibilities. Sometimes something magical will happen in a shot—one of the actors will give this great look—but you can't find a way to use it. So then you have to try to structure the scene so that it can accommodate this shot. Wonderful moments in performance are more important than some kind of structural concept of how the scene should appear. Of course, it depends on how important the concept is and how wonderful the moment is—you have to balance these factors against each other. But sometimes it's worth bending over backwards, even making bad edits, in order to accommodate some little thing that couldn't be anticipated. If the performance is good enough, nobody will notice the bad edit.

When I start working on a scene, the first thing I do is go through each take and pull out the pieces that I like. Once I've done that, I string the pieces together in script order and then begin the process of whittling the scenes down. If I can, I find it valuable to cut a scene using only one type of shot, i.e., all in close-ups, all in medium shots, etc. For instance, I might have a notion that I want to use a wide shot for a certain part of a scene and a close-up for another part. If I make three versions of the scene—the wide, the medium, and the close—I'm able to make a more informed decision. You might have two close-ups that look pretty good, but cutting them together enables you to see these little moments of connection, these little eye looks that make it clear which shot works best.

Another advantage of this approach is that I'm already prepared if Paul comes in and wants to see the scene another way. We can take the photographer's studio scene as an example. For the rough assembly, I began with the camera's POV of Lulu looking directly into the lens. I then used a two-shot up until the kiss, at which time I cut to a tighter two-shot. After the assembly, Paul asked me what would happen if we intercut singles for the earlier section, and I had those edits ready to show him. So this method saved me an enormous amount of time.

On a first attempt, sometimes I'll make my decisions at random, like flipping a coin. I'll work through the scene once, exploring what I think are the best or most consistent options, but while working through it, I'll make note of the other ideas that occur to me. Then I'll go back and do the scene again, sometimes starting from scratch, sometimes altering what I've already done. The more complicated the coverage is, the more options you have to try. You explore those variables until you either run out of time or you decide you've had enough.

RP: When you first read the script, did any potential problems or challenges jump out at you?

TS: The Lulu scenes. We really needed to figure out how to make these scenes work both in the context of the film and as an interesting, coherent narrative in and of themselves. Would it best serve the film to play them realistically—or as more extreme and exaggerated? Was Lulu a real character? Did we even want her to feel like a real character? As Catherine Moore says at one point, "It's all so over the top, but it's about things that are real." We had to walk a fine line.

RP: How did you do it?

TS: My initial approach toward these scenes was to disregard the context and cut them based on the way they were performed and photographed. It's really a matter of selecting the best performance. Once we had the scenes in a shape we felt comfortable with, we plopped them in the film according to the order in which they'd been written. But because the story splits into two parallel parts, it was possible to reshuffle the scenes any way we wanted—you don't have to worry about continuity as much when the characters are on different continents. Even if the order of the scenes seems perfectly fine, you should always consider what would happen if you moved things around. So we tried a lot of different configurations. It was only after we'd put the scenes in context that I started worrying about what to do with them. We ended up changing the dressing-room scene quite dramatically. The entire scene was wonderful, but for the sake of the pacing, we had to cut the first half from the movie.

RP: How did you collaborate with Paul in assembling the final cut?

TS: Before Paul went to Ireland, he gave me some notes with his ideas for rearranging a few things. So when he got back and we began working together in the editing room, the first thing we did was discuss these changes. Then we just started going through the film, scene by scene, from beginning to end. There were quite a few places where we changed the performances because the needs of the scene turned out to be a little different than what I had expected. Generally, the actors were fairly consistent in regard to interpretation, so it was more a matter of selecting the best delivery. We probably changed readings on less than five or ten percent of the lines.

RP: One of the scenes that has been eliminated altogether from the movie is the breakfast scene. Had you anticipated any problems with it?

TS: What made me nervous about that scene was that Izzy does a lot of editorializing. A great deal of the scene isn't about Izzy or Hannah—it isn't about what I did yesterday or what I am going to do tomorrow. It's about the condition of the world, and, while interesting, these are hard lines for an actor to deliver. So it seemed likely that the scene was going to be cut down in some way.

RP: The hospital scene is another scene that has been very much reduced. How did it come to have its present form?

TS: Initially, we tried to make the scene work in the way it had been conceived. But while it was very moving and very powerful, it was not right for the overall pace of the film. It was a slow, talky scene at a point in the film where we needed to be moving forward. Until Izzy finds the dead body, we're just meeting people, and it is always very dangerous to have long, dialogue-heavy scenes before we know where the story is going.

RP: I know there was a lot of debate about how to use the aerial shot in that scene. How did you ultimately decide which shots to use?

TS: They first shot the scene using the overhead shot and the performances changed quite a bit during the subsequent setups. For instance, many of the lines that didn't work in the aerial shot came across very well in the singles. Because it objectifies the viewer, the aerial shot is suited to the sections of the scene that were less emotional and personal. But as we cut those more expositional sections from the film altogether, we wound up using the high-angle shot just as the most visually interesting way to get into the scene. Once we are in the scene, it made no sense to back up to that shot, since that would make you very aware of the editor. The scene was cut to the performances, not to any theory of film structure.

RP: It must become a matter of cinematic instinct . . .

TS: That's all it is. You think about all the different aspects that are important to a scene. Sometimes it's the performances, sometimes it's the visuals, sometimes it's the information conveyed, sometimes it's the pacing. You always have to weigh all the different criteria and figure out what's most important at a particular moment. It's possible to argue almost any position eloquently. That's why ultimately it is Paul's choice. I just give him the best advice I can.

RP: Do you reach a point in the editing process where you don't know what else you can do?

TS: Sure.

RP: And what do you do then?

TS: We screen it. Screening the film not only allows us to see it from a new perspective, but also from the perspective of all kinds of other people. All this input gives you new things to think about.

RP: Would you say that you have a particular style as an editor?

TS: I think it's wrong for an editor to have a style—it depends on the script, the performances, and the photography. I don't impose my own personal style on a film, but rather let the material determine it. On a film like *Sense and Sensibility,* it was important that the photography be beautiful and that the editing be smooth and fluid. Because it is such an emotional story, we wanted to avoid anything that would distract attention away from the narrative. Other films require more vigorous intervention, a more vigorous cinematic style. My goal is just to contribute to the overall look of the film, and to tell the story the best way possible.

RP: Watching the different versions you prepare of a scene, the variations are often scarcely perceptible to my untrained eye. How are you able to work in such detail?

TS: When you're editing, you have no choice but to deal with the film frame by frame—it's not possible to edit a scene any other way. Of course, you look at the overall flow of the film, but you're also dealing with real minutiae—eye moves and things of that nature—that determine where your cuts can go. You can't help but get interested in that kind of thing. Sometimes too interested. You can convince yourself that it makes a difference whether this person raises an eyebrow or not when it really doesn't matter at all. But the cumulative effect of these details on what the scene is trying to say can be tremendous.

RP: Does the detailed way you have to look at the world in the frame spill over into the way you see the world outside?

TS: No. I'm not constantly looking at people's eyelids!

RP: Film editing has undergone a major revolution in the last few years. It used to be that movies were edited by cutting the actual film, but now most movies are edited digitally. The film is transferred to video, which is then fed into the computer and can be manipulated by the editor at the touch of a finger. What are your feelings about this development?

TS: I've worked on the AVID almost exclusively since the summer of 1992. It's changed everything about editing. First of all, on film you can't do multiple versions of the scene and have them all available at the same time. This is partly because you only have one work print, but also because there are just not enough hours in the day. I can work much more quickly on the computer. The speed doesn't help me think any faster, but it does let me see all my options. When cutting on film, if someone had an idea, you would really discuss it thoroughly before trying it out because you knew it would take at least three hours to do, that the work print would be torn apart, and then you would need another hour to put it back together. And of course, there was always the chance you would make a wrong decision. If a director would suggest an idea that I disagreed with, I would have to explain to him very carefully why I thought it was a terrible idea. On the computer, I can just do it, and he can see why it is a terrible idea or I can see that I'm not as smart as I thought I was! Editing digitally allows you to be a lot more daring, flexible, creative—it allows you to try things. You can be a lot more confident that you've made the right choice when you've tried everything you can think of. Also, because the AVID enables you to make a first assembly that's much more presentable, you know that whatever problems you see are real problems, not just the result of loose editing. You're able to make choices based on knowledge rather than speculation.

RP: How do you interpret the story?

TS: Izzy gets shot and, as he lies dying, this vision, fantasy—whatever you want to call it—plays out in his mind. He's very troubled by the way he's lived his life and is looking for some kind of absolution—which he finds through his relationship with Celia. But we never know if Celia even exists or if Izzy just builds a fantasy around the picture of a woman he saw in the bathroom. The film leaves you free to draw your own conclusions about what is real and what's not, about the relationship between dream and reality, fiction and fact. It's a movie within a fantasy within a movie—there are all these levels of reality you have to consider. The only real world is the reality of the people sitting in the theater, watching the movie.

At the end of the film, you're hit both emotionally and intellectually. The scene of Izzy watching the video of Celia sets you off emotionally, but then you have to try to gather yourself together enough to make sense of the finale. At the moment when you are sitting and watching the film, I wonder which experience will win out. I hope that you are jarred intellectually while swept along emotionally. And then, after the film is over and the lights go up, hopefully you will need to think about what you just saw and what it means. Many films contain things worth talking about and revisiting in your mind, but often people aren't motivated to do so. It's late at night and they're concerned with going home and getting on with their lives. A film really has to grab you by the lapels and demand that you think about it, that you talk about it with someone you love. I think *Lulu* is this kind of film.

February 16, 1998

Peter Newman
producer

This was supposed to be the easy one. My partner Greg Johnson and I had just come off of two of the most painful and catastrophic years imaginable. We had foolishly decided to make a $25 million outer space movie in Ireland starring Dennis Hopper called *Space Truckers*. The very mention of doing an outer space movie in Ireland (where no special effects industry exists) brought howls of laughter to everyone we described our plans to. It became only more painful when we found out two weeks before the start of production that $8 million of our Irish investment had mysteriously disappeared, never to return. Spending the next several months trying to find the millions that had gone missing in a foreign land and dealing with other unimaginable disasters took us as near the precipice as producers could ever be taken. Battered, beaten, and broke, I was sure that, if I ever survived *Space Truckers,* I was through with special effects and would never try to make a film in Ireland again.

Somehow we did survive our Irish experience, and after two years of agony we returned to the States. In December 1996, Paul Auster called to say that he was writing a new script called *Lulu on the Bridge* and would like me to consider producing it. This struck me as a god-send. Paul is a good friend, and my respect for his work told me that this would be the perfect next project. *Lulu* was going to be shot in New York, and that meant I wouldn't have to be away from my wife and children for long periods of time. I was sure that I knew how to deal with problems on my "home turf." But the truth was that I didn't think there would be any major problems on this one. No outer space in Ireland. No missing money. No headaches. The optimistic self-denial that I need to produce films had miraculously returned.

I called Paul soon after receiving and reading the script to say that I was definitely in. Here was a gifted artist and a truly honorable man who was offering me a chance to work with him again. We had enjoyed great success, friendship, and fun working together on *Smoke* and *Blue in the Face,* and I was thrilled to have the chance to renew our relationship. I found the script remarkably innovative and complex. I was so moved by the story of Izzy and Celia that I even neglected to focus on the part of the script that dealt with a mysterious glowing stone and the need for special effects. I was anxious to get to work finding the money to produce *Lulu on the Bridge.*

At that early stage, the plan was for Wim Wenders to direct and Juliette Binoche to play the role of Celia/Lulu. The idea was that Wim and Paul would collaborate in more or less the same way that Paul had worked with Wayne Wang on *Smoke* and *Blue in the Face.* As Paul jokingly put it: from WW I to WW II.

There was to be some kind of joint venture between my company, Redeemable Features, and Wim Wenders's producing team. After several fruitful discussions, all the moving parts were coming together. Then, the day before his fiftieth birthday, Paul got a call from Wim— he was having second thoughts. After taking a close look at the project, Wim realized that this would have been his fourth or fifth consecutive movie with a film within the film. Needless to say, Paul was disappointed, but he was also remarkably resilient about proceeding with the project. He called me up and said, "I've got this crazy idea and I don't know how you'll feel about it . . . but I want to direct the movie." I answered, "I'm not saying this because I'm your friend, but I have total belief that you can do this and that you *should* do this!"

Paul had made it clear when he first sent me the script that he had written it not only for Juliette Binoche but for Harvey Keitel in the part of Izzy Maurer. We'd had a talk or two with Harvey about the script when Wim was still signed on as director, and I felt it was very important to find out what Harvey's reaction would be to Paul replacing Wim. I went down to Harvey's office to deliver a new script and I told him, "Before we go any further, I want you to know that

Wim Wenders is no longer involved and that Paul will be the director of *Lulu*." Without missing a beat, Harvey said, "But of course he should direct it." It was a truly wonderful sign of support from Harvey for Paul. While he has a history of discovering and supporting new directors like Quentin Tarantino, Harvey is not an easy person to talk into something. The fact that Harvey so strongly and confidently said, "Of course Paul should direct," was a signal to me that this was a worthy project. I knew that with Harvey's cooperation and support of Paul, we were headed in the right direction.

Soon afterward, Juliette came to New York to do promotional activities for Lancôme. She got together with Paul and reaffirmed her strong support for the project. Paul was in as director. Harvey and Juliette seemed to be in as stars. *Lulu* was getting closer to reality.

With Harvey Keitel and Juliette Binoche's representatives negotiating their contracts, my partners and I went to the American Film Market (AFM) in February 1997 with the idea of finding the proper places to finance *Lulu*. Our thoughts were to go to the same foreign distributors who had been most successful in marketing *Smoke* and *Blue in the Face*. Not only did they have a creative appreciation of Paul's work, but they had also made a substantial amount of money selling the films in their home territories. We felt that it was only proper to give them the first chance to buy *Lulu*.

Smoke and *Blue in the Face* had turned out to be tremendous creative and business successes internationally. Besides the overall popularity of the work of people like Wayne Wang, Harvey Keitel, and William Hurt, we were particularly impressed by the unbelievable support of Paul Auster's work overseas. While his books sell in healthy amounts in the United States, in countries like France, Italy, Germany, Spain, and Japan, he is a top-ten writer, an extremely well-known figure. There was a huge built-in audience for anything that Paul Auster would do in the film arena the next time out.

At the AFM, the only distributor to read the script and say "I'm in no matter what" was Fabienne Vonier of Pyramide, the French distributor of *Smoke* and *Blue in the Face*. In France, *Smoke* had done over one million admissions. Considering that France is one-fifth the size of the United States, that's fairly extraordinary. The numbers were reflective of Paul's massive popularity there—and also of how well Pyramide had marketed the film. Fabienne was now the first investor to believe in *Lulu*.

We also sought out foreign sales agents to see who could advance the remainder of the budget, the amount not taken care of by our sale to the French. We circulated the script discreetly among three or four companies that sell international rights. The most aggressive and passionate was Capitol Films of London, which is run by Sharon Harel and Jane Barclay. They were quality people with an impressive record who had previously invested in and sold films such as Roman Polanski's *Death and the Maiden* and *Hoop Dreams*. Despite the amount of work they had at the AFM, Sharon and Jane managed to read the script within forty-eight hours and get on a plane to New York to lock us in our office. They said they wouldn't let us out until *Lulu* was theirs. Eight hours later we closed a deal that made them the international sales agent for the movie. It was early March and *Lulu* was financed. Maybe.

When things are going smoothly, there's usually reason to worry. In late March, Juliette Binoche won the Academy Award for Best Supporting Actress. I'll never forget watching her hug her agent on television, feeling so happy for her, and then, all of a sudden, thinking, "Oh my God. This means she's not going to do *Lulu*." In the film business, once someone wins a big award, all bets are off. Our Keitel/Binoche quiniela was definitely on the ropes.

My conversations with Binoche's representatives became increasingly vague. We eventually got to the point in May where brochures had to be printed for our sales effort at the Cannes Film Festival. Much to Harvey's credit, even though we didn't have a signed deal with him yet, he said, "By all means, use my name, go out there and publicize it," but Juliette was still on the fence. We printed an insert so that if at the last second she had said she would be in the movie, we could add it to this beautiful brochure that Capitol had provided.

As an added plus, Paul just happened to be on the jury at Cannes last year. It kept him tremendously busy, but it helped that he was there. There was a tremendous amount of desire for the project. Each prospective buyer had the same two questions. Number one was, "Yes, we know Paul Auster is a great writer, but can he direct?" Whenever we could get Paul out of jury meetings or screenings to introduce him to all the territorial distributors, his intelligence, passion, and charisma helped to persuade these people that he really did have the focus and ability to make a movie.

The second question concerned who the leading actress was going to be. As we were really unable to say who it would be, we kept buttoning our lips.

A couple of weeks later, it turned out that Juliette was not going to be in the film. Nevertheless, Paul and I both agreed that we were going to make the movie—no matter what. But we needed a lucky break.

When one spends a lot of time with Paul, one realizes that, much as in his novels, there are weird sets of occurrences, strange things that keep happening to him. Those occurrences seem to happen for a reason. So the fact that Mira Sorvino was on the jury with Paul at Cannes seemed more than just a coincidence. We had worked with Mira in *Blue in the Face* and had great respect for her as an actress. After hearing the bad news from Juliette, we started to make lists of appropriate replacements for her. In late May, we had preliminary conversations with Mira's representatives about the film. In July, Paul and I sat down to lunch with Mira to say how much we wanted her to play Celia. She read the script, thought about it, and came back very quickly—within ten days—to say that she would love to do it. *Lulu* was alive and well.

We just kept moving along. From the very first day, Paul and I kept repeating our mantra: we know we're making the movie, we know we're making the movie, we know we're making the movie. . . . We had Mira, Harvey, and the money. As a producer, my real responsibilities now focused on getting the remainder of the cast and crew together. Because Paul was, in the strictest definition, a first-time director, it was important that he have very experienced people with him. I was happy that Kalina Ivanov, who had worked on *Smoke* and

Blue in the Face, would be his designer. We eventually found Ang Lee's editor, Tim Squyres, and that excited me as well. We hired a very steady line producer in Amy Kaufman, and she proceeded to assemble a top-level crew. I was particularly happy to be working with the incredibly talented costume designer, Adelle Lutz. When all those people were in, it made me even more confident about Paul's choice of Alik Sakharov as director of photography. While he was not by any means a novice, Alik did not have an extensive list of feature film credits. But I could hear that the passion and simpatico between Paul and him was very strong, and I wanted to support that. Paul's hunches were more than correct; Alik gave *Lulu* a remarkable and beautiful look.

In the world of independent film financing, until you have 100 percent of the money, you don't have a dime. Whoever invests in or buys a movie insists that the producers get a type of insurance called a completion bond. It guarantees that the producers will be monitored to prove that they have the wherewithal to finish the movie. A producer may have contracts in front of him that say he has $9 million, but he doesn't have access to any of that money until a completion bond insurance company approves them. Our bond was with a company called Film Finances, which is backed by Lloyds of London. In order for our $9 million to be released, the bank loaning us the money first needed the completion bond to be in place. To put it mildly, there were a lot of negotiations and intricacies involved in unlocking that money. From the time when Mira first said she was going to be in the movie, it took four or five months to turn the paper commitments from our foreign buyers into real money for the movie. Our legal bills were going through the roof, people were getting nervous, and we still had immense amounts of work to do to prepare *Lulu* for production.

There was the need to cast the rest of the movie, which has over thirty interesting speaking parts. It's a great thing for a producer when the writer/director is so respected that you don't necessarily have to go through the agents but can have the director pick up the phone and call actors himself. I had previously had experiences like that working with people like Robert Altman and Jonathan Demme. They could pick up a phone, say to a particular actor, "I'd like you to be in my movie," and get the response, "I'm in, no matter what." I found that Paul had that level of respect among the acting community, and people like Vanessa Redgrave, Mandy Patinkin, Jared Harris, and Gina Gershon wanted to be in the movie as soon as Paul called.

There was also a tremendous amount of organizational work to be done. During the next several months, it was a constant process of trying to get the budget and the schedule to such a level that we could make the best possible movie and still afford to complete it if anything went wrong. I had to deal with the scary proposition of getting a special effects house to create the glowing stone at virtually no cost. And just in case I hadn't experienced enough pain yet—Paul wanted to shoot the bridge scene in Ireland.

On August 25, we began preproduction. Although the bank loan did not go through until the night before production, we somehow managed to scrape together enough money to keep the necessities moving ahead. The casting was completed, the crew was fully hired, and we were looking forward to a start date of October 20. It seemed that everything was finally in place.

It is standard procedure for a film and its producers to have a working relationship with all the talent and craft unions. In recent years, it has become a much easier proposition in New York to make a deal with the unions that work behind the camera. The last deal to come together always seems to be the one with the Screen Actors' Guild (SAG). Independent producers are required to put up a bond to guarantee that the actors will receive their full salary even if the production should collapse or the financing not fully materialize. Over the last twenty years, I had routinely negotiated the standard terms of the bond with SAG—and I was expecting this to be an easy discussion regarding *Lulu*. Again, I was horribly wrong.

One week before production, we received a letter from SAG unlike anything I'd encountered before. They had decided—for the first time in my experience—to enforce the issue of advances against foreign residuals. This involves the money that would be collected for the actors two or three years after the release of the film on television and home video in foreign countries. It was SAG's opinion that the producers had to put up in an escrow account money sufficient to pay the actors for those residuals when they would be due—some time after the year 2002. SAG was taking the position that unless the producers put $500,000 in a bank account in the next five days, they were going to call a strike against *Lulu* and prohibit their members from acting in it. I couldn't believe that this was happening, and I certainly didn't have $500,000. Out of all the occupational groups that we had dealt fairly and reasonably with in the past, the actors were number one. It had always been a point of honor with us, and we have rigorously shared our profits with the actors who appear in our films—*Smoke* and *Blue in the Face* being a good example. A very heated weeklong discussion ensued between our company and SAG—with very little movement on either side. It seemed inconceivable that an independent production that was employing over thirty actors, many of whom would not ordinarily be working in film, was being threatened by their own union! But the time bomb continued to tick.

The night before our first day of photography, October 20, I received a phone call from SAG informing us that we had one day to sort out our problems before they would shut down the film. It was the worst kind of irony that after all we had endured over the past year, *Lulu* was going to fall apart because the actors' own union wanted to shut us down. Part of me thought it was a bluff, but considering we were borrowing $9 million from a bank, it was a bluff we had to take seriously. The heat continued from SAG on the first day of filming. Their new threat was a shutdown in two days, but first they needed to advise the members of their guild of what was about to happen. On the second day of photography, Harvey Keitel was in his trailer preparing to do one of the most difficult scenes in the movie, the death scene. I was advised that a representative of SAG was on the set and knocking on Harvey's door. She wanted to inform him that he would have to go on strike and walk a picket line in two days. Harvey was absolutely incredulous. He could not believe that his own union was interfering with his preparations for this demanding scene—and with his strong desire to work on a film that meant so much to him. The SAG functionary left the trailer in a state of both contrition and embarrassment. Every night for five weeks, there was the threat that we could be shut down the next day. We had to work under immense pressure and uncertainty while keeping the full extent of our problems away from Paul and the cast and crew. It was not until the sixth week of production, literally day 35 of the shoot, that we finally managed to come to some sort of economic settlement with SAG.

All of our problems regarding the actors seemed to have passed and the filming was going magnificently. We had known for the last year that Paul intended to have the writer Salman Rushdie play the part of Harvey Keitel's interrogator, who was then named Dr. Singh. On the advice of our insurance company, we did not notify the majority of the cast or crew about his involvement until two weeks before his appearance, in order to minimalize the risk of a planned action against Mr. Rushdie. We all felt that Rushdie's presence in the film would have great impact, not only because of how well-suited he was to the role, but also because of the statement it made about freedom of expression. When word got out, a certain segment of the crew was up in arms. A number of them declared that they would refuse to work if he was hired. I fully understood their fears and safety concerns, but I was sure they were overreacting. Once again, events proved me wrong.

There began an eye-opening series of meeting with Rushdie's security people, as well as with representatives of the city and federal government. I learned about everything from anthrax attacks to terrorist bombs. In the end, the experts could only guarantee an 80 percent chance of safety. Even to a crazed gambler, those were distressing odds. It was with great regret that five days before his start date, Paul and I had to tell Salman that he was out of the film.

Luckily, on extremely short notice we were able to get Willem Dafoe to step in and do the part. Not only did Willem accept within twenty-four hours of receiving the script, but he gave a brilliant performance. We had dodged another bullet.

The last day of photography in the U.S. was a very emotional

scene that we filmed in Sunset Park, Brooklyn. Izzy was escaping from the room where he'd been imprisoned by Dr. Van Horn. After his last shot, we had a little ceremony and presented Harvey with the saxophone that he'd played as Izzy Maurer in the film. The tough man broke down and cried. The crew also presented him with a very special gift: they mooned him with the words "Good-bye Izzy" painted in blue on their bottoms.

Then came Ireland. In light of what had happened the last time we had been there with *Space Truckers*, I feared we were tempting fate by returning. Of course, the weather that weekend in Dublin was the worst it had been in a decade, and it was only through the miraculous efforts of cast and crew that *Lulu* was able to wrap on schedule.

Principal photography was completed in Ireland on January 4, 1998. Paul Auster had done an extraordinary job as a director. Now it was time for him to fashion the best possible film with his editor, Tim Squyres. In the twelve months and ten days since Paul first called me, *Lulu* had taken every possible body blow and survived. We had lost our first director and leading lady. We had waited until the first day of principal photography for our money. SAG had threatened to strike, and the risk of terrorism had cost us the services of Salman Rushdie. We had created the glowing stone effect successfully at a reasonable cost. We had even survived Ireland. Auster's baby was alive and well. It will be incredibly interesting to see how she grows up.

February 25, 1998

All photographs are by Abbot Genser, except for those on pages iv, 122, and 124, which are by Pat Redmond.

PAUL AUSTER'S eight novels, including *New York Trilogy*, are canonical reading for fans of American literature all over the world. Auster wrote the screenplay for the internationally acclaimed film *Smoke* and also wrote and codirected its companion film, *Blue in the Face*. He lives in Brooklyn, New York.

REBECCA PRIME received her B.A. in English literature from Columbia University in 1996. She worked as a production assistant on *Lulu on the Bridge*.